The Macat Library

世界思想宝库钥匙丛书

解析马塞尔·莫斯
《礼物》

AN ANALYSIS OF
MARCEL MAUSS'S
THE GIFT

Elizabeth Whitaker ◎ 著

韩蒙 ◎ 译

上海外语教育出版社
外教社 SHANGHAI FOREIGN LANGUAGE EDUCATION PRESS

MACAT

目　录

CONTENTS

引 言

要 点

- 马塞尔·莫斯（1872—1950）是一位法国社会学家，以其对社会行为研究的贡献、学术合作和政治活动而闻名。
- 《礼物》一书表明，互惠*式的交换行为（如礼物交换）是社会关系的体现，这种关系通过延伸至未来的义务将个人与群体联结起来。
- 《礼物》一书所描述的民族志*内容（即民族研究和文化研究的深度）别具一格，研究结果意义非凡，该书与社会科学、政治学和个人生活之间的关系也独有特色。

马塞尔·莫斯其人

马塞尔·莫斯，《礼物》（1923—1924）一书的作者，1872 年出生于法国东北部的埃皮纳勒。离开大学后，他成为法国社会学*（研究社会行为的学科）领域的一名重要人物，其影响力达半个世纪之久。莫斯一生中大部分时间用于与其他学者合作、参与社会学项目的研究以及担任专业期刊的编辑。他在政治上非常活跃，参加了合作社运动*（运动理念为支持企业应为工作者集体所有），出版社会主义*（社会主义的一般原则是每个人在权力和金钱的分配中都有一定的份额）著作。莫斯反对反犹主义*——一种对犹太人的偏见——以及政治权力的滥用。他能说多门语言，也能够阅读古希腊语、拉丁语和梵语文献。

在研习哲学和法律之后，莫斯与其舅舅埃米尔·涂尔干*开始密切合作，后者颇具声望，被称为"法国社会学之父"；两人有着共同的研究兴趣：通过分析文化*信仰、法律体系及社会制度*来研究人们的思维方式。

1917 年涂尔干逝世后，莫斯接手了他 20 年前创立的期刊《社会学年鉴》*。莫斯的著作《礼物》首次刊登于 1923—1924 年版的《社会学年鉴》，探讨了涂尔干社会学理论、古代法律与人类学家（以古今世界各地的人类为研究对象的学者）收集的最新数据之间的关系。这部著作重点论述了人际交往中持续性与非持续性的物质交换行为间存在的差异，并思考了经济活动、社会行为、信仰体系和道德观念之间的关系。

《礼物》的主要内容

《礼物：古式社会中交换的形式与理由》一书认为，无论是有意识的还是无意识的，人们都不会在缺乏回报预期的情况下有所付出。书中分析着眼于古式社会*中实体物品、人和无形商品的赠予和接受情况（莫斯使用"古式"一词来定义无货币流通却存在贸易*和以物易物*的土著社会和古代社会）。所有这些社会形态中不仅存在日常的经济往来，还有周期性更长、范围更广的礼尚往来现象。莫斯专注于其中互惠式的交换行为，因为这一行为能将个体和群体联系在一起，建立起长期关系。他的研究重点放在某些社会形态上——在这些社会形态下，从财产到头衔的所有东西"都可以进行传递，并用于资产平衡"。[1]

莫斯强调经济系统与社会系统、政治和道德之间的交融。他分析了明确的法律规定和社会习俗如何约束小型、熟人型社会中的交换行为，并指出早期的礼物交换体系中有相似的范式，且这些范式在工业化社会中得以"幸存"。通过观察，莫斯最后得出结论，从人类学视角观照经济学意义上的交换行为，会为公共政策的制定带来一定启发。他也认为，对制度化的互惠形式（互换原则）进行分析并拓展其应用范围可能会产生更公平的政治经济体系。

《礼物》一书内容翔实，莫斯结合了特定的社会、历史和文化背景，分析了各个社会形态下的礼物交换规则，这体现出他的研究立场：他坚信研究应给予社会各方面因素以同等程度的重视，换言之，物质因素和技术因素的研究与宗教及道德信仰的研究同样重要。《礼物》也展示了社会系统和文化信仰是如何塑造了人类行为并赋予其意义。这些想法也贯穿于莫斯关于宗教、季节性 *（社会活动根据季节变化而产生的变化）和人格 *（人作为独立个体的观念）的作品中。

《礼物》是莫斯最知名的作品，也是他为数不多的独立作品之一。他的思想传播途径之一是与同事进行交流，紧接着，这些思想又通过与其他人的交流进一步传播开来。但假如他不寻求合著的话，他的影响力将会更为深远。两位人类学历史学家在评估莫斯的影响时指出"莫斯的作品分布过于零散，且大部分篇幅很短，多为合著。如果他的作品能够以更紧凑的形式出现，他的名气会更大一些。尽管当今的社会科学成就或多或少都体现着他的思考结果，他不凡成就的价值仍旧难以评估。"[2]

莫斯的这部短篇作品对学术界和文学界产生了巨大的影响。该书已有三个英译本，2015 年版为最新版。它仍是社会学和人类学 *的关键文本，继续为人文科学（语言、文学、哲学等领域）和社会科学（历史、经济学、政治学等领域）提供创作灵感。

《礼物》的学术价值

《礼物》可用于分析任何环境中的经济行为。它为分析人类活动的动机以及理解经济学概念——如理性*（经济行为中，人们如何通过推理权衡成本和收益以做出最佳决策）和效用*（任何购买的物品的实用性）——提供了独到见解。该书还探讨了经济学和社会文化系统间的相互影响，也涉及了法律规范和政治哲学的相关研究，从而为理解不同数据背后的共同主题提供了指导。《礼物》的最后一部分阐释了重大事件对知识界的影响。莫斯试图分析第一次世界大战*后欧洲的动荡政局。他对西方社会的推论与当时的伦理关切息息相关，如今仍存争议。

《礼物》思考了不同文化背景下礼物馈赠行为的意义，并就其纯粹的交易功能背后金融意义的缺失给出了自己的看法。该书还揭示了赠予、接受和回馈行为中存在着互相矛盾的价值杂糅现象，如在互惠式的交换行为中，慷慨和无私的品质伴随着利己行为和约束性的义务。

《礼物》详述了那些在我们自己的社会中发生的、被假定为完全出于无私的礼物馈赠行为，莫斯认为这些行为包含着更简单社会形式下的价值观和期望值：在每个人的生活和工作中，恩惠和资源的付出都需要回报；这样的资料转换巩固了人际关系，并带来了名誉和地位。

与此同时，《礼物》还表明，商业交易与人际关系并非完全脱节。货币本身是一种文化产品，产生于特定的社会和法律框架之下。该书解释了为什么单靠金钱无法弥补有偿劳动的贡献——劳动者投入到工作中的不只有劳动，还有才能、创造力、智慧和知识等。同样，工作绩效体现在多个层面，仅凭金融指标难以一概而论。另外，该书还阐明了人类消费行为带来的影响，并就此展开讨论，对"个体以独立的方式行动和思考"这一假设提出了质疑。

《礼物》是一本适合所有学科的书。书中只透彻分析了某一主题，而这一主题与人类生存的普遍主题紧密相关。无论是作为个人生活中的一环，还是作为理论分析的焦点，互惠式礼物交换都是具备不确定含义的人类行为。该书持久的生命力也证明了人类的社交互动存在着永恒的魅力。

---

1. 马塞尔·莫斯：《礼物：古式社会中交换的形式与理由》，伦敦：劳特利奇出版社，1990年，第14页。

2. 保罗·博安南和马克·格莱泽编：《人类学的高光时刻》，纽约：艾尔弗雷德·A.克诺夫出版社，1988年，第264页。

第一部分：学术渊源

1 作者生平与历史背景

要点 &—

- 马塞尔·莫斯的《礼物》对人类学家和其他学者进行文化分析的方法产生了持久的影响。他们所分析的文化中，经济、政治、技术和个人动机等各种因素是交织在一起的。

- 莫斯在社会学（对社会行为、社会制度、人类社会起源和组织方式的研究）、法律、宗教和语言领域所接受的学术训练为他进行包括礼物交换在内的文化系统比较分析*（通过比较不同的系统、人工制品或特征进行的研究）提供了得天独厚的准备条件。

- 20世纪初政局动荡，正是在这样的背景下，莫斯开始着手分析民族学*相关资料（对生活在自身特定环境中的族群进行研究所获得的信息）及其对工业化社会的影响。

为何要读这部著作？

马塞尔·莫斯在《礼物：古式社会中交换的形式与理由》中谈到了一个直入人心的话题：社会关系。[1]另一个问题是，相较于受社会和文化的控制，个人能在多大程度上决定自己的思想和行为？该书探讨了上述两个问题，并在学术层面对人类的群居生活方式进行了阐述。

莫斯探讨了赠送礼物和回赠礼物的行为是如何使人们介入那些受规则管理和文化价值熏陶的交换循环的。他收集了不同文化背景下的数据资料，进行统一阐释，将他的舅舅、社会学先驱涂尔干所创立的社会学研究方法发扬光大。《礼物》一书打开了思想史的一扇窗，向读者介绍了大量令人着迷的民族志细节，同时也概述了一种比较分析的研究方法，为探索互惠式交换（简而言之，是一种相互交换的体系）和社会凝聚力（一个运作良好的社会所具备的稳定性特征）之间的关联提供了思路。莫斯还思考了这一针对小型熟人社会形态的研究为修正工业化社会的经济体系、实现共同利益带来了哪些方面的启示。

与早期学者不同，莫斯认为经济、政治、宗教、亲缘关系 *（某一民族在形式上辨识不同人际关系的方法）等体系并不是孤立存在的。与涂尔干的理论思想一脉相承，莫斯关注社会共识和制度化的规则程序，正是这些元素构成了个体信仰与行为的语境。莫斯没有将生态因素或物质条件的限制等任何单一因素当作社会文化系统发展的主导力量。虽然他认为社会不断发展、日渐复杂，但他清楚地表明复杂的社会形态并不一定比简单的更好。

莫斯将他和涂尔干的想法传递给了他的同行及年纪较轻的同辈，如著名法国人类学家克劳德·列维-斯特劳斯 * 以及他的学生们，其中包括精神分析学家和人类学家乔治·德弗罗 *、非洲人类学先驱丹尼丝·波尔姆 * 和电影制作人兼人类学家让·鲁什 *。通过他们，莫斯还影响到了思想家皮埃尔·布尔迪厄 *、乔治·孔多米纳 * 以及其他许多人。[2]

> "人类学是他（莫斯）再满意不过的部分了，自此之后（一切研究）都难以企及，他的这部作品把（人类学研究）向前推进了一大步。"
>
> —— 玛丽·道格拉斯 *："前言：没有免费的礼物"，载《礼物》

作者生平

马塞尔·莫斯 1872 年出生于法国东北部洛林大区的埃皮纳勒，其父母均从事纺织业。虽然莫斯出身于正统犹太家族，但他并不信奉宗教。他的亲戚中有许多学者，其中最著名的是他的舅舅、社会学之父埃米尔·涂尔干。莫斯的表妹（涂尔干的侄女）、海洋生物学家克劳德特·拉斐尔·布洛赫，是英国人类学家莫里斯·布洛赫*（1939 年出生）的母亲。

莫斯的大学时光是在波尔多度过的，他的舅舅也在那里任职，是担任法国历史上第一位社会学和教育学教授。1895 年莫斯搬到巴黎继续他的学业。他花了两年时间（1897—1898）在英国和荷兰旅行，回到巴黎后，莫斯从 1900 年开始在巴黎高等研究实践学院讲学，1930 年后在法兰西学院讲学。

莫斯成年后便积极投身于让整个欧洲都为之头疼的政治运动。他参加了集体主义*学生运动，加入了法国工人党*和革命社会主义工人党*，上述均是左翼运动及左翼组织。他还为《社会主义生活》《人性》《社会主义运动》等左翼出版物撰写文章。莫斯撰文支持小说家兼剧作家埃米尔·左拉*，左拉对法国军队中弥漫的反犹主义（反犹情绪）以及艾尔弗雷德·德雷福斯*审判中法律程序遭受军事干涉一事进行了公开批评，这迫使当局撤销了对德雷福斯的指控。莫斯一生致力于反对反犹主义和种族主义，他的作品（包括《礼物》在内）都具有非常明显的政治意识和政治维度。[3]

1917 年涂尔干去世，他作为教育学（教学方法和实践）教授在法国帮助实施的课程变革遭到清算。莫斯这位涂尔干社会学方法的倡导者也退回到行政岗位，接管了由涂尔干于 1898 年创立的期刊《社会学年鉴》。第一次世界大战（1914—1918）期间他失去了包括社会学家亨利·伯夏*和罗伯特·赫兹*在内的多名期刊撰稿人。1925—1926年，莫斯与民族志学者保罗·里韦*和社会学家吕西安·莱维-布吕尔*在巴黎大学共同创办了民族学研究所。莫斯在此授课并参与管理，直到1939年。第二次世界大战*（1939—1945）中莫斯损失更为惨重，加上个人和家庭的问题，他郁郁寡欢，停止了学术研究工作，于1950年在巴黎去世。[4]

创作背景

马塞尔·莫斯是一位研究广博、训练有素的学者，他学习了多门语言，包括俄语、希腊语、梵语、拉丁语、马来-波利尼西亚语。在波尔多大学时，他研习过哲学和法律。1895年在公务员考试中获得第三名后，莫斯选择在巴黎高等研究实践学院，一所法国公共财政资助的、具有选拔性质的学术科研机构，继续深造。在这里，莫斯研究了比较宗教学以及古希腊、古罗马、古印度和日耳曼民族的文学哲学作品。1897—1898年，他前往荷兰和英国，并与英国首位人类学教授爱德华·伯内特·泰勒*进行了短暂的合作。泰勒从整体*出发为"文化"一词下的定义——文化中各个组成部分相互依赖——至今仍被引用，但我们引用时需注意这一定义有可能发生的变化。[5]

1902—1930年间，莫斯在高等研究实践学院教授课程"未开化民族的宗教历史"。1930—1939年间，他在法国另一所享有盛名的高等学府法兰西学院开设了相同的课程。[6]他对比较宗教学长期保有研究兴趣，这对其研究礼物交换这一社会现象也有一定的帮助。

两次世界大战之间的早几年，莫斯作为一名社会主义者，以法国合作社运动（在这场运动中，公司由工人集体所有）成员的身份继续研究政治哲学。在《礼物》中，莫斯坚持个人主义是促进生产活动、提高社会参与度的推进器，但他也指出，商品交易若脱离了其道德和社会背景，则有可能成为剥削行为。

---

1. 马塞尔·莫斯：《礼物：古式社会中交换的形式与理由》，伦敦：劳特利奇出版社，1990 年。

2. 玛丽·道格拉斯："前言：没有免费的礼物"，载马塞尔·莫斯著，《礼物》，伦敦：劳特利奇出版社，2000 年；沃尔特·戈尔德施密特："对马塞尔·莫斯《礼物》的评论"，《美国人类学家》第 57 卷，1955 年第 6 期，第 1299—1300 页；赛斯·里柯克："马塞尔·莫斯的民族学理论"，《美国人类学家》第 56 卷，1954年，第 58—71 页。

3. 马赛尔·富尼耶：《马塞尔·莫斯传》，新泽西州普林斯顿：普林斯顿大学出版社，2005 年，第 4 页。

4. 保罗·博安南和马克·格莱泽编：《人类学的高光时刻》，纽约：艾尔弗雷德·A. 克诺夫出版社，1988 年，第 264—266 页；沃尔特·戈尔德施密特："对《礼物》的评论"，第 1299 页；赛斯·里柯克："马塞尔·莫斯的民族学理论"，第 58—59、64—65 页。

5. "从广泛的民族志意义上看，文化或文明是一个复杂的整体，包括知识、信仰、艺术、道德、法律、习俗以及人类作为社会成员所获取的任何其他能力和习惯。"爱德华·伯内特·泰勒：《原始文化：神话、哲学、宗教、艺术和习俗发展之研究》，伦敦：约翰·默里出版社，1871 年，第 1 页。

6. 列维-斯特劳斯接替莫斯在巴黎高等研究实践学院任教后，将课程重新命名为"无文字民族的宗教比较学"。

2 学术背景

要点 &⊷

- 人类学是对人类生物学历史、文化学历史以及当前人类变化的研究。《礼物》对礼物交换进行了比较研究，其作为一种核心制度——从习俗活动的角度来说——构建了人际关系并引导了商品、人力和无形资产（如仪式、头衔等）的流动。

- 20世纪初期，社会学家（研究社会历史和结构的学者）和人类学家着力于对非西方社会的形态特征进行记录，并根据社会进化阶段论*（根据社会进化原则，人类的技术、社会发展和智识水平会经由一系列固定的发展阶段而日趋完善，从而实现社会形态的整体进化）对信息进行分类和理解。

- 莫斯与社会学家保罗·福科内*和埃米尔·涂尔干等学者合作，探索了文化制度的主要范式。

著作语境

马塞尔·莫斯撰写《礼物》时，其叔父涂尔干的学说在法国盛行一时，当时正值世纪之交，法国哲学对英国功利主义*——一种哲学传统，也是一种推崇自由主义*的政治传统，认为个人理性是推动现代经济生活积极向好的基本力量——十分排斥。[1]法国哲学家认为，激进的个人主义未能解释个人行为和信仰产生的社会背景。也就是说，功利主义的观点忽视了经济组织和社会组织之间的关系，忽视了文化信仰和社会地位对个人选择的影响。包括亚历克西·德·托克维尔*在内的法国哲学家认为，激进的个人主义产生剥削，导致人们为社会所异化，并脱离政治生活。

涂尔干的观点介于"个体与社会分离"与"个体完全受社会环境的控制"两者之间。虽然评论家经常评论说个体在其社会学体系中并不重要，但涂尔干对不同类型的社会结构下政治体系和社会制度对个体人格自由发展的容许度非常感兴趣。涂尔干专注于发掘社会成员共识中的规范和规则，并评估它们对个人选择的影响。他没有忽视个人意志的力量，但作为一名社会学家，他的任务是解释社会运行的各种内在力量并确定其集体表征*（社会成员的共同的信仰和对事物的共同理解）。1901年，莫斯与社会学家保罗·福科内合作，为法国《大百科全书》撰写了一篇文章，文章阐述了涂尔干的理论方法。[2]

虽然研究素材来自小型的、非西方的社会形态，但莫斯认为自己是一名社会学家。法国社会学一直将人类学视为其下属的一门学科，尽管后者很久以前就已在其他地方成为一门独立学科。[3]在英美两国，人类学关注所有社会形态特别是非西方社会形态间的比较研究，而社会学则倾向于关注工业化社会的内部运作机制。

> "在我们的社会形态诞生之前所形成的经济和法律体系中，个体间达成的交易里几乎不存在任何形式的货物、财富或产品交换行为。首先，是集体而不是个体将交换和缔结契约作为彼此之间应尽的义务……而且，他们交换的不仅仅是资产和财富、动产和不动产以及经济学意义上"有用的东西"。值得一提的是，这种交换是为了表现礼貌……最后，尽管人们通过自愿赠送礼物的方式来完成呈献和回献，但其归根结底是强制性的，违者会引发私人或公共领域的冲突。"
>
> ——马塞尔·莫斯：《礼物：古式社会中交换的形式与理由》

学科概览

涂尔干 1897 年出版的《论自杀》一书说明了社会力量对个体行为的影响（莫斯负责编制资料）。[4]通过设定社会群体、国家和时间三个变量，涂尔干分析了自杀率的变化。分析表明，精神痛苦并非仅仅因生物因素或偶然因素而随机产生。书中还阐述了涂尔干的经典分析方法：从实证方法*出发，客观地对系统的各种复杂性进行详细审视（"实证"研究指通过观察以可验证的论据为基础的研究）。莫斯也继承了这一分析方法。同时，涂尔干和莫斯认识到，他们对其他文化的阐释会受到自身所秉承的集体表征和政治经济制度的影响，这一点是领先于时代的。

莫斯对社会进化论持怀疑态度，由此可见涂尔干和莫斯在这方面还是非常谨慎的。莫斯认为，尽管方式不同，但所有社会形态都是文明的。[5]这明显偏离了 19 世纪和 20 世纪早期的探险家、传教士以及如英国哲学家赫伯特·斯宾塞*、美国人类学家路易斯·亨利·摩尔根*等理论家所信奉的社会进化逻辑。他们认为社会形态可以像动物物种一样，按照复杂度和完美度，由低到高进行排序。[6]为了阐明自己的观点，莫斯提到，散布于太平洋的一些社会形态中存在着相似的礼物交换行为，而非洲、亚洲和美洲地区也存在着类似的系统。但在《礼物》中，他拒绝就不同社会中的类似习俗是传播引入还是独立产生的争议发表看法。[7]

莫斯还是按照近似于进化程度高低的顺序，对其研究所聚焦的现存古式社会形态进行了排序。他还研究了现代印欧社会之前的社会形态，并试图在当今的习俗中寻找"幸存者"（即从古代社交行为中延续下来的某些习俗特征）。在此基础上，他提出了一个原始社会管理经济交换行为的模型。但莫斯发现，在社会进化的三个阶段中基本原则是同样适用的，因此不同社会形态之间并没有高低优劣之分。

学术渊源

在莫斯进行创作的那个年代，人类学已经从案头研究转向了田野调查。在人类学家实地调查作品的基础上，如布罗尼斯拉夫·马林诺夫斯基*对太平洋特罗布里恩群岛的调查和弗朗兹·博厄斯*对北美西北海岸的调查，《礼物》的写作成为可能。莫斯对材料的处理方式受到了多方面影响。在波尔多时，他受到了哲学家艾尔弗雷德·维克托·埃斯皮纳斯*和奥克特·哈梅林*的影响，前者研究了技术和文化传统及形式背后的集体智慧，后者的研究旨趣在于人际关系的约束效果。[8]莫斯亦与涂尔干以及其他原创撰稿成员通力合作促成了颇具影响力的期刊《社会学年鉴》。

虽然莫斯赞同流行的观点，即研究更简单或更"原始"的社会运作形式是有用的，因为它们显示了之后复杂社会形式的一些基本特征，但他不同意人们（包括摩尔根在内）认为的"文明总是向前向上发展，按照蒙昧期—野蛮期—文明期的顺序发展。"的说法。[9]同样，莫斯在巴黎高等研究实践学院开设的比较宗教学课程偏离了苏格兰人类学家詹姆斯·弗雷泽*在 12 卷《金枝》中总结出的人类学基本教义。[10]弗雷泽相信，人类的思想是从原始巫术发展到宗教，最后才发展成为科学的。他排斥"类同性"*（"物以类聚"的原理）和"接触"*（原始巫术中，神秘力量存在于如人体产物之类的物品，并可被操纵用于巫术），以期实现对因果关系的真正理解。莫斯拒绝接受弗雷泽的理论框架以及他的民族学比较方法（对特定民族进行系统研究后，再将研究资料进行比较），因为弗雷泽使用的材料片段脱离实际语境，属人为拼凑，以满足研究目的。[11]

莫斯的方法是系统性的，以证据为基础。像博厄斯一样，他拒绝自上而下以逻辑演绎的方式，研究进化、心理、地理、种族或经济因素对社会系统和个体行为的影响。[12] 莫斯更认同涂尔干的研究方法：从案例内部出发或通过案例比较，找寻出可以确定人类行为尺度的政治—法律制度、社会体系及共同信念，在莫斯看来，这些因素只能为人们的行为划定界限，并不能决定人们的行为。

1. 玛丽·道格拉斯："前言：没有免费的礼物"，载马塞尔·莫斯著，《礼物》，伦敦：劳特利奇出版社，2000 年。

2. 保罗·福科内和马塞尔·莫斯："社会学：对象与方法"，《大百科全书》第 30 卷，1901 年，第 165—176 页。

3. 赛斯·里柯克："马塞尔·莫斯的民族学理论"，《美国人类学家》第 56 卷，1954 年，第 60 页。

4. 埃米尔·涂尔干：《论自杀》，伦敦：企鹅出版社，2006 年。

5. 里柯克："马塞尔·莫斯的民族学理论"，第 60 页。

6. 路易斯·亨利·摩尔根：《古代社会：从蒙昧期至野蛮期再到文明期的人类进化路径研究》，纽约：亨利·霍尔特出版社，1877 年。

7. 马塞尔·莫斯：《礼物：古式社会中交换的形式与理由》，伦敦：劳特利奇出版社，1990 年，第 97—98 页。

8. 保罗·博安南和马克·格莱泽编：《人类学的高光时刻》，纽约：艾尔弗雷德·A. 克诺夫出版社，1988 年，第 264 页。

9. 例如，摩尔根非常肯定人类社会自蒙昧期至野蛮期到文明期的演进顺序，从而在没有实证论据的情况下创立了分类范畴。他认为人们迟早会找到相应的社会习俗或亲缘体系来填补论据上的空白。摩尔根：《古代社会》。

10. 詹姆斯·乔治·弗雷泽:《金枝》,纽约:西蒙和舒斯特出版公司,1996年。

11. 马塞尔·莫斯:"高等研究院:未开化民族的宗教史教学",《宗教史回顾》第45卷,1902年,第36—55页;弗雷德里克·巴特等:《人类学的四大传统:英国、德国、法国和美国的人类学》,芝加哥:芝加哥大学出版社,2005年;里柯克:"马塞尔·莫斯的民族学理论",第61页。

12. 弗朗兹·博厄斯:《种族、语言和文化》,伦敦:科利尔-麦克米伦出版社,1940年。

3 主导命题

要点 🔑

- 莫斯撰写《礼物》的那个年代，社会学家试图解决的首要问题是社会的组织方式以及社会结构是如何与其运作方式关联在一起的。

- 一些学者认为社会发展是通过技术层面、社会层面和智识层面的一系列有序进步而实现的；对于其他学者来说，社会形式是由物质、技术或生物因素决定的；还有一些学者仍然专注于记录具有历史和地域特殊性的语言、习俗和生活方式。

- 莫斯专注于同等社会发展水平下财产、人员和服务的交换方式。他试图从个案中寻找规律但选择在语境中理解个案，而不考虑根本原因。

核心问题

　　马塞尔·莫斯在《礼物》中提出的核心问题是：在一个没有货币和合同法的社会中，交换的目的、意义是什么？合法的交换秩序又是什么？莫斯发现，民族志学者——从事民族及其文化研究的学者——经常感到困惑的一点是，古式社会（土著或类似土著的已绝迹的社会形式）成员在赠送、接受及偿还礼物时都遵循着严格的规则。旁观者似乎不曾注意到，交换行为包含时间维度，还涉及相互勾连的道德因素和物质资料的转移，如果对此做一描述，社会轮廓、等级分布、动态和凝聚力等状况便一览无余。

　　交换这一主题与涂尔干感兴趣的个体性问题是有所关联的。涂尔干和莫斯都认为个体人格在最简单的社会形态中相对不发达，因为在这种社会形式下，家庭或氏族＊（共有一个祖先的亲族）就是一切，而团结——互相联结——是"机械的"，或者说是工作和任务专业化程度较低的必然结果。工业化社会则走向另一个极端：个体人格地位过高；社会中个体之间的联系无处不在，但人们却并不承认这一点。由于专业职能相互依赖，社会成员得以"有机"地团结起来。在这里，最重要的是个性，而不是氏族的归属感。[1]

虽然涂尔干认为，处于两种极端社会形式之间的个体人格仍受限于密集的社会关系网和文化信仰，但莫斯表明，社会个体还是会在声望、名誉及其带来的物质利益的混合驱动下进行礼物交换。这是一种利己行为。此外，即便没有市场交易（即纯粹根据商定价值进行物品交换的情境），这种互动活动总的来说也代表了一种一贯的、可预见的体系。虽说无论是哪种情况，交换行为都与个体的具体情况有关，但互惠式的给予行为是公开的，因此对公平性的要求更加严格，而市场交换则是隐性的，从而与个人和群体名誉渐行渐远。

莫斯总结道，从根本上说，我们都是一样的——只是社会背景的差异才使我们行为各异。因此，差异只是程度上的区分，而非性质上的。他认为市场经济＊为主导的社会应该为个人利益和集体福祉考虑，重新强调经济交换中互相制衡的各个要素。[2]

> "主题已很鲜明。在斯堪的纳维亚文明以及许多其他文明中，交换和缔结契约总以礼物的形式发生。它们理论上是自愿行为，但实际上，送礼和回礼都是义务性的。"
>
> ——马塞尔·莫斯：《礼物：古式社会中交换的形式与理由》

参与者

在整个学术生涯中，莫斯一直与其他学者有着密切合作。他的作品展示出一种博采众长却又特立独行的思想轨迹。《礼物》就是这样的例子。

《原始分类》是莫斯1903年与涂尔干合著的一篇文章，它探讨了简单社会形态下对物品、人和现象的分类方式。[3]莫斯与涂尔干提出，逻辑范畴与社会分类之间存在联系，例如男女之间或氏族与部落*（一个围绕着亲缘关系和阶级而形成的、具有政治属性的社会群体）之间的联系。换句话说，概念上或语言上的类别并不存在于事物的自然属性之中，而是社会的产物。

莫斯和涂尔干将这些想法扩展为一套关于"神圣*之物"（值得宗教崇拜的思想、仪式和物体）的、不断发展的理论。涂尔干1912年关于比较宗教学的著作《宗教生活的基本形式》探讨了社会如何在"图腾"*——某些无生命的事物，其概念上可转化为具有神秘力量的神圣事物——中实现自我象征，从而将社会属性的范畴映射到自然界。[4]莫斯与历史学家、社会学家亨利·于贝尔*于1899年撰写的关于古印度和早期犹太教动物献祭的文章《献祭的性质与功能》确定了"神圣之物"的概念，赋予了献祭之物要求神灵回赠礼物的权力。[5]他们1904年出版的《巫术的一般理论》则侧重于介绍波利尼西亚*和澳大利亚-美拉尼西亚*地区的 **mana***。[6] **mana** 是一种可移动的超自然力量，遍及宇宙，依附于物体，并通过某些人群的优势和力量展现出来。[7]

莫斯于1906年与社会学家亨利·伯夏合写了一篇关于爱斯基摩人*（因纽特人）迁徙的文章《论爱斯基摩人社会的季节性变化：

社会形态学研究》。莫斯在文章中表明，爱斯基摩人族群冬季抱团和夏季分散的习俗不能用简单的生态学术语来解释，例如捕获动物的机会。[8] 两人认为，这一原则也同样适用于解释其他族群活动的季节性变化。这篇文章促进了后续一系列作品的诞生，这些作品确立了人类信仰和实践的社会起源，而在其他学者看来，人类的信仰和实践是生物需求、普遍心理结构或自然物理定律导致的结果。

当时的论战

《礼物》中的分析以多位学者研究为基础，其中包括布罗尼斯拉夫·马林诺夫斯基对太平洋特罗布里恩群岛的调查，英国哲学家、人类学家 A. R. 拉德克利夫-布朗 * 对安达曼群岛和西澳大利亚的调查以及德裔美籍人类学家博厄斯对北美西北海岸的调查。[9] 这些民族志学家对人类学和社会学的发展产生了深远的影响。

拉德克利夫-布朗借鉴了涂尔干关于集体表征和社会制度的思想，发展了英国结构功能主义 *。[10] 结构功能主义将社会比作人体，个人的意志或行为——这里比作细胞——不会从根本上改变系统，至少不会通过自己的力量加以改变。马林诺夫斯基与拉德克利夫-布朗一起创立了英国社会人类学（人类社会的比较分析），这种思想与结构功能主义不同，它非常重视个人作用，认为社会起源于人类基本的生理和心理需求。[11]

博厄斯采用了一种不同的民族志方法，称为历史特殊论 *。他避免理论演绎，支持全面的数据收集和对土著 * 语言（某地首批居民所说的语言）的深入研究。[12] 通过使用实证论据如亲缘系统（定义人们何以相互关联的系统）、艺术形式甚至头部形状等，他展现出社会的变化状况，并在此过程中挑战了流行的种族理论、进化理论以及"社会形态通过内部变量进行自动调节而逐步趋稳"的观点。[13]

　　莫斯对礼物交换的分析结合了上述这些观点，他理所当然地以结构功能主义为前提，但也考虑到了社会个体的动机。他同博厄斯一样，并不赞成"某些社会或习俗优于其他社会或习俗"的观点。他在具体的社会语境中审视社会制度，注意变化，不对因果关系（即一个或多个变量直接产生特定的结果）发表确定的看法。与此同时，莫斯还关注文化之间的相似性，以便为人类社会的一般规律提供论据，证明人类社会的进化是从简单社会到复杂社会的松散演进过程。

---

1. 埃米尔·涂尔干：《社会分工论》，纽约：自由出版社，1984 年。

2. 马塞尔·莫斯：《礼物：古式社会中交换的形式与理由》，伦敦：劳特利奇出版社，1990 年。

3. 埃米尔·涂尔干和马塞尔·莫斯：《原始分类》，芝加哥：芝加哥大学出版社，1963 年。

4. 埃米尔·涂尔干：《宗教生活的基本形式》，纽约：自由出版社，1915 年。

5. 马塞尔·莫斯和亨利·于贝尔："献祭的性质与功能"，《社会学年鉴》，1897—1898 年，第 29—138 页。

6. 马塞尔·莫斯和亨利·于贝尔：《巫术的一般理论》，伦敦：劳特利奇出版社，2001 年。

7. 涂尔干：《宗教生活的基本形式》，第 223 页。

8. 马塞尔·莫斯和亨利·伯夏：《论爱斯基摩人社会的季节性变化：社会形态学研究》，伦敦：劳特利奇出版社，1979 年。

9.《礼物》问世的三年前，马林诺夫斯基发表了关于特罗布里恩群岛岛际交换关系的论文。同年，拉德克利夫-布朗发表了完成于约 15 年前的安达曼群岛田野调查报告；十年前，拉德克利夫-布朗发表了西澳大利亚的田野调查报告。从 19 世纪末到 1940 年，博厄斯发表了一系列关于北美西北海岸族群的文章和专著。

10. A. R. 拉德克利夫-布朗：《安达曼岛人》，剑桥：剑桥大学出版社，1933 年。

11. 布罗尼斯拉夫·马林诺夫斯基：《西太平洋上的航海者：美拉尼西亚新几内亚群岛的土著经济活动和探险》，伦敦：劳特利奇出版社，1922 年。

12. 弗朗兹·博厄斯："人类学比较方法的局限性"，《科学》第 4 卷，1896 年第 103 期，第 901—908 页；弗朗兹·博厄斯："移民后代体形的变化"，《美国人类学家》第 14 卷，1912 年第 3 期，第 530—562 页。

13. 参见博厄斯关于北美西北海岸部落中父系和母系亲属关系的讨论，弗朗兹·博厄斯：《夸扣特尔人的民族学》，芝加哥：芝加哥大学出版社，1966 年。

4 作者贡献

要点 &

- 莫斯认为，没有现代通货*（现金或贝壳之类的交换媒介）流通的社会仍然拥有法律、政治和经济体系来规范商品和服务的流转。

- 莫斯从道德和物质层面解释了熟人社会的交换行为，在多种多样的民族志研究中提炼出它们的共同点，并总结出一个模型用于理解大众社会中的人际互动现象。

- 比较分析需要对两个以上的案例进行比对，以确定相似点和不同点，用以解释各自的结果。该分析将关于社会制度（法制化的关系或活动）和集体表征（社会成员的共同信仰和对事物的共同理解）的最新理论观点与当代实证研究和比较分析的方法结合了起来。

作者目标

莫斯撰写《礼物》的目的是解释礼物交换在简单社会形态中产生的约束性义务。为此，他将其他学者收集的民族志证据与他自己对古代语言和哲学的研究相结合，侧重分析不同社会形态中交换行为准则的共同特征。

莫斯表明，简单社会形态下已存在规则来规范所有有形和无形的贵重物品的转移。礼物交换机制与婚姻或宗教活动等其他社会机制有关，有助于社会团结（社会成员间的互相支持和联系）和稳定。莫斯从法律、社会、政治和道德层面审视经济学意义上的交换行为，帮助人们从新的视角理解效用（经济学中，购买商品对购买者的物质效用或心理效用）和理性利己性（做决定时对成本和收益的衡量）这两个概念。参与礼物交换既是自愿的，也是强制性的；

既是有益的，也是昂贵的；既有物质层面的意味，也有精神层面的考量。莫斯还表明，简单社会和复杂社会的经济交换体系并无本质差别，均是按照类似的原则进行运作。复杂社会中也残存着简单社会中更具社会意义的经济交换行为。

《礼物》的结构清晰地反映出作者的目的和研究方法。莫斯首先描述了全世界小型社会中施—受或互惠行为（指行为和有形礼物都应以正式或循环的方式得到回赠这一原则）的基本体系。之后，他分析了一种极具竞争性的体系，其特点是"内置升级"——每件礼物的价值都要高于前一件，而不是等值——乃至通过毁坏财物的方式来显示社会地位。他向读者展示了现代社会的语言、法律和习俗中也幸存着的、与礼物交换相似的、从古代文明延续下来的实践活动。最后，莫斯对现代政治经济体系的失败之处做出了评判，并思考了我们可以从简单社会形态中学到些什么来保障社会福利，改善人际关系。

通过撰写《礼物》一书，莫斯的主要目标得以实现。他的主要论点得到了大量实证论据（可通过观察证实的证据）的支持。然而，由于缺乏工业化社会的相关数据参照，他的结论中推测的成分会更多一些。

> "物品的流通，包括男人、女人、儿童、宴会、典礼、仪式、舞蹈的流通，甚至是玩笑和辱骂的流通。总而言之，他们的本质都是相同的。人之所以要送礼并得到回赠，是为了给予或受到他人'尊重'——我们称之为'礼节'。但从另一方面来说，人们在给予别人礼物的同时，也把自己送了出去；之所以如此，是因为所欠于别人的正是他'自己'——他本身和他的财物。"
>
> —— 马塞尔·莫斯：《礼物：古式社会中交换的形式与理由》

研究方法

为了分析社会进化的中期阶段（社会形态在一些可辨识的层面上变得更加复杂），莫斯假设，在社会形成早期阶段，个体完全从属于家庭或氏族。群体通过**总体呈献制度**相互绑定，包括他们之间可交换的所有事物：商品、礼节、配偶、膳食以及舞蹈、头衔、名字和仪式等无形资产。

莫斯解释说，现在和古式社会的礼物交换体系是从总体呈献制度发展而来。而这些社会的领土范围更大，政治单元（如部落）更具规制，贸易（根据规定的价值标准，正式交换不同物品）、以物易物（当场交换不同的物品，可能有讨价还价的过程）伴随着礼物交换现象的发生而发生，反映出个体人格的逐步显现。在复杂的农业和工业社会中，随着以抽象货币为中介的现代匿名交易的兴起，家庭和社会约束逐渐减弱，个体性得到进一步发展。[1]

莫斯通过波利尼西亚、澳大利亚和新西兰、马来西亚、欧亚大陆极北地区、非洲和美洲的感恩节盛宴和礼物献祭等例阐释了总体呈献制度。他随后描述了一类竞争性礼物交换循环现象，并以北美西北海岸的"**夸富宴**"* 来命名。这是一种展示财富的手段，交换的礼物价值越来越大，有时甚至还会被毁掉。

按照莫斯的阐释，类似的体系在巴布亚新几内亚独立国和美拉尼西亚等地也很常见。此外，许多体系看似是总体呈献体系的初级版本，实际上都是以"内置升级"为标志的中间阶段。[2] 这种温和的**夸富宴**体系存在于澳大利亚、斐济、南亚和莫斯所谓的俾格米人* 族群中。古罗马、古印度、古日耳曼民族以及古代中国的法律和习俗中也有这种体系的痕迹。[3]

最后，莫斯分析了古代闪米特文明、希腊文明、罗马文明、印度文明、日耳曼文明、凯尔特文明和中华文明的语言及法律中的"幸存物"（古代思想或实践的存留踪迹）。他表明，互惠行为和社会制度仍旧通过礼物交换的方式维持着旧有的义务和权利体系。然而，在复杂社会中，货币和契约规则的出现使礼物交换正规化，成为社会主要的交换形式，个体性也因此占据了上风。

时代贡献

莫斯的分析为理解不同民族背景下的礼物交换和社会关系提供了新颖的观点。为了进一步说明，他对其称之为"竞争式总体呈献"的竞争式"内置升级"的宴会和礼物体系进行了统一解释。这其中就包括"**库拉***圈"（特罗布里恩群岛之间的财富流通形式）和北美西北海岸的"**夸富宴**"体系。

根据马林诺夫斯基的描述，"库拉圈"中流通的物品包括经过装饰的白色贝壳臂章和红色贝壳项圈，它们通过在特罗布里恩群岛间往返的独木舟流转。[4] 日常商品可用以物易物的方式交换，但只有礼物才具有无形的超自然属性，能够赋予收礼者以声望而非使用价值，收礼者则要在收礼一段时间后回赠礼物。臂章和项圈的价值会因为被受人尊敬的"大人物"拥有过而上升，这与它们自身的美观性毫无关系。

博厄斯笔下北美西北海岸"夸富宴"中的礼物也同样带有超自然力量。在这个体系中，铜是特别受重视的，因为它可以换取其他的铜制品。"夸富宴"的特别之处在于其极端强调竞争。人们为了真正"压垮"参与斗争的部落及其首领，可能会毁掉自己大量宝贵的财产，如毯子、食物、房屋，甚至把铜制品扔进大海。莫斯通过这个例子展示了无法归还的礼物是如何羞辱收礼人从而提高送礼者的声望的。[5]

　　根据莫斯的描述，礼物循环方式虽有不同，但其代表的物质资料和道德元素的转移模式却是相同的。他发现，在简单社会中，一次性商品交易与涉及个人以及更多社会元素的礼物交换就已经存在明显区别。[6]莫斯的比较分析表明，所有社会形态中，各类转移都是有序且存在意义的。

---

1. 马塞尔·莫斯：《礼物：古式社会中交换的形式与理由》，伦敦：劳特利奇出版社，1990年，第5—6、46、82—83页。
2. 莫斯：《礼物》，第7页。
3. 莫斯：《礼物》，第7、19、97—98页。
4. 布罗尼斯拉夫·马林诺夫斯基：《西太平洋上的航海者：美拉尼西亚新几内亚群岛的土著经济活动和探险》，伦敦：劳特利奇出版社，1922年。
5. 莫斯：《礼物》，第37、74、86—88页。
6. 莫斯：《礼物》，第11页。

第二部分：学术思想

5 思想主脉

要点 🔑

- 莫斯表明，赠送礼物不仅是因为送礼者慷慨大方，它还是建立社会关系的工具。礼物交换背后的社会义务以积极或消极的方式将人们联系在一起。

- 礼物交换使熟人社会得以正常运作：它促进了经济、社会、宗教、政治生活的建构。礼物互赠中互赠双方相互产生义务，或礼物赠送者通过礼物获得接收者的名誉和地位。

- 莫斯展示了互惠式交换如何在保护个人和群体自主性的同时，对双方产生约束，相比之下，商业交易更容易形成剥削关系。两者之间的平衡影响了社会凝聚力程度和人际互动的质量。

核心主题

莫斯《礼物》的重点分析对象是全世界（尤其是美拉尼西亚、北美西北部和古欧亚大陆＊）的小型社会或古式社会。他描述了必要的赠礼、收礼以及在一段时间后的回礼是如何以积极或消极的方式联结个人与群体、维持长期社会关系的。礼物交换的动力源自虽不成文但仍可作为正式裁判依据的法律原则、与名誉和声望相关的文化信仰以及在各方之间传递的有形及无形之物所承载的象征意义。物质、人以及巫术或超自然力量等元素的混合使得经济活动成为社会、宗教、政治制度中不可或缺的一部分。

整个礼物交换体系背后的基本原则是"好有好报"或互惠互利的概念，通俗的说法则是"天下没有免费午餐"。这些从早期欧美历史文化中传承下来的思想似乎表明，无论人们生活在什么样的社会，送礼都是一个复杂的过程。礼物不只是一个有形物体，其本身混合了各式各样的信息。例如，即使是单独的词"gift"和"present"，其本身也可指时间和知识（或天赋，如音乐才能）一类的馈赠物。

莫斯专注于研究互惠行为如何提高小型熟人社会形态下的社会凝聚力。与计算劳动力、土地、商品和服务价值的市场化社会形态不同，小型熟人社会中的礼物交换更多体现的是个人和社会层面上的意义。熟人社会中的交换行为进一步受到诸如声望、责任、名誉、祭祀、为人是否慷慨大方和自身利益等因素的影响。可供交换的物品包括有形商品（珠宝、家居用品和服装等实物）、各方经常共享的食物和饮料以及无形的事物，如好客、舞蹈、姓名、头衔和宗教仪式等。回赠的礼物可能完全不同于收到的赠礼，但其价值必须等同于收到的礼物，甚至更好。在所有的情形下，人们都是根据既定体系计算礼物价值，有时考虑实用性，有时不考虑。这些条款规则形象地勾勒出某一社会形态的大致图景，并展现出这一社会形态与其他社会形态之间的联系。[1]

> "在那些落后社会或古式社会中，究竟怎样的法律规约及利益规则让回赠礼物变成了义务？送出的礼物中究竟蕴含着怎样的力量，促使礼物接受者必须回馈？"
> —— 马塞尔·莫斯：《礼物：古代社会中交换行为的形式和原因》

思想探究

基于对礼物交换的分析，莫斯认为文化在塑造人类行为方面起着重要作用。与当时流行的"社会特征由生态、物质和生物因素决定"的观念相反，莫斯关注的是社会制度以及文化信仰或集体表征（社会成员的共同信仰和对事物的共同理解）对社会的作用，就像他早期关于巫术与宗教的作品中所描述的那样。通过分析礼物交换的"整体社会现象"或"整体社会事实"，莫斯阐述了涂尔干的观点，即简单社会形态下的制度有助于维护社会稳定和团结。因此，为保证社会凝聚力（社会成员之间的亲密度），个体需通过长期系统地履行对他人的义务，以实现对自身行为的约束。然而，互惠式交换仍然允许个体追求自身利益。

尽管礼物交换的循环揭示并加剧了社会内部及社会之间的等级落差和不平等现象，但它仍是小型熟人社会的聚合剂。持续性的互惠交换与非持续性的销售截然不同。非持续性的销售指通过货币交易或无货币交易实现的以物易物（现场交换不同的物品）或贸易（根据规定的价值标准，正式交换不同物品）。换句话说，两者的区别在于，互惠交换在时间上是开放的，交换物品的价值估算不以货币价值为标尺，而非持续性的销售是一次性交换，交换双方的价值是平衡的，例如，一定数量的香蕉等值于一定数量的贝壳，或有其他通货来衡量商品价值。莫斯还认为，贸易在简单社会中并非无迹可循，信用这一概念就像利息一样，通过提升价值和延迟回馈的方式进入礼物交换的循环。总之，在所有社会形态下，包括礼物交换在内的经济活动都是根据相似的原则构建的。

莫斯认为，比较各种社会形态下礼物交换的异同之处，对我们所有人而言都具有指导意义，它指引我们建构一个更加美好的社会形态。这也意味着，进步并非都会带来积极效果。[2] 在先进文明中，经济学被视为直接与现金和合同挂钩的学问，人们尚不能认识到互惠行为的重要性，遑论着力培养。莫斯提到，西方社会中的人更加孤立，而简单社会中的人相互联系更加密切，但仍然保持着各自的自主性。重点是，无论是在物质交换的层面还是非物质交换的层面，西方的社会制度都没有尽最大的可能促进互惠式交换的发展。结果，人们彼此之间的距离越来越远，社会团结程度也越来越低。莫斯很欣赏那些简单社会中"已经学会如何在不牺牲自己利益的前提下表示反对和赞同"的族群，他总结说："未来，我们所谓的文明世界的任何阶级、国家和个人都必须了解（这种互惠式交换）。这是他们长葆智慧和团结的秘密之一。"[3]

语言表述

《礼物》大约有一百页的正文以及同等篇幅的注释，看似是一篇简短的文章，它在 1923—1924 年初次发表于《社会学年鉴》。随着包括期刊创始人涂尔干在内的几位主要撰稿人的离世，该期刊自第一次世界大战以来一直处于停滞状态。莫斯曾经就多个项目与撰稿团队进行过合作，他决心将离世学者的学术遗产发扬光大。如果这些学者依旧健在的话，便可见证莫斯对复兴《社会学年鉴》所做的贡献。

《礼物》一书最开始的标题是《论说礼物：古式社会中交换的形式与理由》。莫斯选用了"论说"这个字眼，反映出他打算以简洁有序而不过于学术的方式提出论点。但这本著作的受众是对 20 世纪早期社会学和人类学有基本了解的读者。对于如今的读者来说，事先掌握一些书中讨论的当代社会学理论和民族志内容对阅读该书是有帮助的，但并非必要。书中的注释可以帮助读者弥补这一缺失。

1954 年的英译本，行文多为当时的正式书面语，相比起来，本书分析中引用的 1990 年译本，无论在内容还是气质上，与原文的契合度都要稍逊一筹。[4]

---

1. 玛丽·道格拉斯："前言：没有免费的礼物"，载马塞尔·莫斯著，《礼物》，伦敦：劳特利奇出版社，2000 年，第 viii 页。
2. 马塞尔·莫斯：《礼物：古式社会中交换的形式与理由》，伦敦：劳特利奇出版社，1990 年，第 77 页。
3. 莫斯：《礼物》，第 82—83 页。
4. 请参见两个译本对莫斯以 "Les clans, les âges et, généralement, les sexes." 开头的句子处理。马塞尔·莫斯："论说礼物：古式社会中交换的形式与理由"，《社会学年鉴》，1923—1924 年第 1 期，第 97 页；马塞尔·莫斯：《礼物：古式社会中交换的形式与功能》，伊利诺伊州格兰克：自由出版社，1954 年，第 70 页；马塞尔·莫斯：《礼物：古式社会中交换的形式与理由》，伦敦：劳特利奇出版社，1990 年，第 72 页。

6 思想支脉

要点 🔑━

- 除了发现礼物交换具有建立政治法律体系、维系社会关系的功能，莫斯还认定礼物具备一种促使人们将其保留在流通领域的超自然特质（一种无法只用物理名词进行量化描述的特质）。

- 文化信仰中，礼物的神秘属性有利于社会成员遵守规则，维持社会团结和稳定。虽然互惠式交换可以维系社会内部和社会之间的等级制度，但有超自然力量参与的礼物循环需要向不富裕阶层倾斜，以缓解社会不公带来的影响。

- 莫斯表明，礼物与商业交易的超自然元素在复杂社会中依然存在。他提供了一个模型，这一模型可用于调查各地经济活动中隐含的动机和含义。

其他思想

在《礼物》一书中，莫斯提出，太平洋的波利尼西亚和美拉尼西亚地区存在着"mana"，"mana"在其他古式社会形态中的变体解释了古式文化将礼物与宗教、精神和巫术力量融合在一起的方式。在 1904 年出版的，与历史学家、社会学家亨利·于贝尔合写的《巫术的一般理论》一书中，莫斯将"mana"这一概念解释为弥漫在宇宙中的超自然力量。[1] 遍观南太平洋、非洲、亚洲、美洲及中东的古式社会，社会成员之所以能获得权力和优越条件，是因为"mana"依附于物品和财产并经由这些器物传递给人。为了描述这种类似"mana"的属性，莫斯介绍了毛利人*——新西兰土著——观念中的"hau"*，"hau"指的是一种礼物拥有的、可以将自身带回原地的力量。当社会中的政治法律体系、名誉、社会地位都不起作用时，反而是礼物因其本身的超自然力量而可以保证其继续流通。[2]

莫斯认为，上述观念中的礼物与救济品（用于布施的礼物）有相似之处，二者都可被看作有神灵参与的礼物交换，他在 1898 年与亨利·于贝尔合作撰写的《献祭的性质与功能》一文中谈及了神灵这一主题，这篇文章主要探讨了古代宗教中祭祀的作用。[3] 正如人类向神灵献祭可以换取神灵的恩赐并为自身谋求长远利益一样，通过施舍穷人，富人清楚意识到自身在物品交换流通中的位置才是财运的来源。莫斯还提出，基督教、伊斯兰教、东北非国家苏丹的豪萨族（撒哈拉以南某民族）、古代闪米特人、印度教以及阿拉伯文化都将布施视为实现社会正义、履行社会义务的一条原则，拒绝布施之人将会遭受天谴。

莫斯通过描述"mana"和"hau"等概念以及它们与布施的关系，将神灵当作礼物交换过程中的润滑剂，为其提出的"礼物流通本质上是一种义务"的观点提供了论据支撑。莫斯认为应该提醒工业社会中的富裕阶层应始终记得庇护不富裕阶层。只有对财富进行再分配，过于富足的物质生活才能得到神灵佑护。

> *"因此，若法律，尤其是回赠的义务，没有被履行，（毛利人的礼物）中就会含有这种力量。"*
>
> —— 马塞尔·莫斯：《礼物：古式社会中交换的形式与理由》

思想探究

按照莫斯的解释，礼物是鲜活的存在，它们带着前任主人的印记继续自己的流通之旅。他通过分析毛利人口中的"hau"来说明这一观点。"hau"主要与一种被称为"taonga"的物品相关，"taonga"是母系一方流传下来的、可用于礼物交换的财产，如垫子、装饰品和护身符等。这些"taonga"都是与其来源地有固定联结的财产，与之相对的"oloa"则指的是像工具一样、与其来源地没有固定联结的财产。虽然在日常交易中，"taonga"可用于交换其他物品，如食物等，然而，若"taonga"被作为礼物赠送出去，"hau"的力量会迫使收礼者回赠礼物，而不服从的人则会受到严重的（可能致命的）伤害。

"taonga"的生命力来自"其所在地的丛林、荒野和土壤中的'hau'"。[4]此外，"taonga"也承载着赠送者的部分生命，"'taonga'，或者说是'taonga'自身带着的'hau'……会一直追随着它的使用者们，直到使用者通过宴席、节庆或者回赠礼物的方式回报以等值或者更高价值的礼物。反过来看，之后收到'taonga'再将其送出的人会获得比前一位送出者更高的权威和权力，那么对于'taonga'的第一位赠送者（也是最后一位获赠者）而言，他会是这一礼物循环中最有地位的人。这似乎成了主导萨摩亚和新西兰地区财富、贡品和礼物进行义务性流通的关键思想。"[5]

莫斯认为，在简单社会中，礼物**具有鲜活的生命**，而不仅仅是某种象征。他提及古印度法律时解释说，"此外，土地、食物和所有赠送者给出的东西都被进一步人格化了，它们是鲜活的生命，是能交流的对话者，是可缔结契约的对象。它们在主动寻找被赠出的机会。"[6]

同样，在德国和法国，一份关于售卖和贷款的合同，往往会附上一件几乎不怎么值钱、但"带有赠送者个人色彩"的个人物品，这件物品会在交易完成后归还原主。[7] 这一习俗源自早先的传统，即将某一信物切成两半，由缔约双方分别保管，以便双方相互制衡。

这些例子都证明了莫斯的观点，即礼物的超自然属性提供了法律规约所不具备的东西，它是一种心理动机，一种根深蒂固的对超自然力量的敬畏之情。

被忽视之处

莫斯提出了主要理论框架用以分析互惠式交换背后的法律和文化体系，而他提出的"我们所处的世界（包括礼物在内）充斥着神秘力量"这一观点却并没有像前者一样被读者热情接纳，其中一个原因是《礼物》中关于如"mana""hau"一类概念的证据相对较少。[8] 另一方面则是由于西方社会的科学研究思维和一神论宗教信仰——对单一神的信仰——与超自然的世界观截然相反。而西方盛行的世界观与功利主义是一致的。功利主义是由英国哲学家杰里米·边沁*创立的哲学理论，与哲学家约翰·斯图亚特·穆勒*极度重视个体潜力和责任的观点联系紧密。功利主义坚信，利己的人类本性会促使人们基于效用（即根据选择带来的实际后果，权衡成本和利益并做出决定）的考量而做出理性选择。除非受到社会或国家的干涉，个体行为必定会促进增长，提供更多的机会，造福全民。[9]

涂尔干和莫斯拒绝采用功利主义的视角，他们更加关注社会的力量。通过他们的方法，效用和理性在不同的文化背景下可以有不同的定义，有些文化背景下，它们还用来解释社会和超自然力量之间的关系。从那时起，在大众文化和政治哲学的思潮中，功利主义的影响起起伏伏。它在新自由主义经济学派（20 世纪晚期 21 世纪初期盛行的一种重新强调 19 世纪自由主义的经济哲学理论，支持通过自由市场和法治而非个人的自由行为来促进经济增长）和新形式的社会达尔文主义（以进化论解释生理上的优劣何以为不同的个人或群体带来不同的特征和命运）中获得新生。这些观点形成的前提是假设人性可以通过自身利益来定义，以及市场交换天然带有功利性的色彩，或从某种程度上来说，市场经济本质上是在参与者个人利益的驱动下而运作的。

虽然人们认为莫斯关于互惠式交换中的神秘元素的见解不是他的主要观点，但它们并没有完全被忽视。正如莫斯所指出的那样，学者和评论家会研究为什么有些富人会给慈善机构捐款，并花大价钱购置艺术品和其他非功利性财产。他们质疑这种炫耀性消费与美国社会学家、经济学家索尔斯坦·凡勃伦＊所描述的 19 世纪的阶级跃迁有关。[10] 研究人员还认定器官捐赠行为中存在某些超自然的或与巫术有关的观念，因为人体器官通常被认为是携带有捐赠者个体人格的生命体，因此这种生物性的赠予将义务施加给了接受者及其家属。[11]

---

1. 马塞尔·莫斯和亨利·于贝尔：《巫术的一般理论》，伦敦：劳特利奇出版社，2001 年。

2. 马塞尔·莫斯：《礼物：古式社会中交换的形式与理由》，伦敦：劳特利奇出版社，1990 年，第 8—13 页。

3. 马塞尔·莫斯和亨利·于贝尔："献祭的性质与功能"，《社会学年鉴》，1897——1898年，第29——138页。

4. 莫斯：《礼物》，第11——12页。

5. 莫斯：《礼物》，第12页。

6. 莫斯：《礼物》，第56页。

7. 莫斯：《礼物》，第62页。

8. 赛斯·里柯克："马塞尔·莫斯的民族学理论"，《美国人类学家》第56卷，1954年，第63——64页。

9. 马歇尔·萨林斯：《人性的西方幻象：对西方悠久历史中等级制度、平等思想及无政府主义崇拜的反思，以及对其他人类状况概念的比较》，芝加哥：仙人掌出版社，2008年。

10. 索尔斯坦·凡勃伦：《有闲阶级论：关于制度的经济研究》，纽约：麦克米伦出版社，1899年。

11. 莱斯利·夏普："商品化的亲属关系：美国器官捐赠者的死亡、哀悼以及遗体所有权的争夺"，《美国人类学家》第103卷，2001年第1期，第112——133页。

7 历史成就

要点 🔑

- 莫斯表明，礼物流通循环中固有的约束性义务映射着未来的社会关系。经济交易具有文化意义，受到社会规约管束，他将这一原则的应用范围从无钱币社会拓展到了以市场经济为运作基础（基于既定价值的商品交换）的社会。

- 莫斯阅读古代律法文献的原文，并将自己的理解与其他学者的民族志研究结合在一起进行分析。

- 莫斯将现有社会和古式社会中的礼物流通和商业交易形式进行比较，得出了令人信服的分析。但由于缺乏相关的实证数据，他对工业化社会的含蓄分析似乎并不那样可靠。

观点评价

《礼物》中，莫斯对各小型社会的互惠式交换体系进行了比较，展示了集体表征（社会成员的共同信仰和对事物的共同理解）和社会制度（制度化的社会关系或活动，如退休或婚姻）是如何以特定方式界定社交活动、引导人类行为的：除了法律框架，礼物背后的道德和神秘力量也可以确保它们在预定的时间框架下，回到赠送者手中或者被继续传递下去，自身价值还会得到一定抬升；贸易和以物易物随着"总体呈献系统"（即合乎习俗的付款行为）的出现而出现；毯子、鱼、山药和铜器等商品相互之间的价值比是固定的，因此回赠行为可能存在一定的滞后性；在某些情况下，会有如贝壳、金属碎片或者在个人或氏族间流通的硬币之类的通货充当交换媒介；所有这些中小型社会形态都存在如购买力、债务和信贷这样的概念，就像现代社会一样。[1]

反之亦然：在现代市场经济中，古式社会中的礼物流通方式仍然存在。这在各项法律、文献中均显而易见，受邀请者有回请义务也可以体现这一现象。它解释了赌博行为和其他一些交换行为为何会牵涉名誉，为何会包含理论上自愿但实际上是义务性的支付行为。它还解释了"天下没有免费的午餐"[2]这个事实。

然而现如今，通过税收和立法程序进行的社会财富再分配使得旧有的、事关个人名誉的物品交换循环被打断了。另外，随着匿名交易（与个人身份和名誉无关的交易方式）不再被简单视为抛开文化价值观的个体理性选择的结果，当下对消费行为象征意义和社会意义的评估也变得困难起来。同样，该书也缺乏足够的证据证明，与商业交易相比，礼物交换的比例越高，社会凝聚程度也越高。

这些限制条件意味着莫斯只能为现代世界提供建议。他建议将古式社会可借鉴之处与个体性、市场原则和工作意愿结合起来进行考虑。通过这种方式，复杂社会体系可以阻止对穷人的剥削，通过社会保障更充分地补偿劳动者，并承认在礼物交换过程中双方完全履行约束性义务是不可能的，甚至是不可取的。[3]

> "早在人类知道如何签字之前，就已经学会了如何以自己的姓名和名誉做担保了。"
>
> —— 马塞尔·莫斯：《礼物：古式社会中交换的形式与理由》

当时的成就

在莫斯之前，也有学者将经济交换行为视为由文化信仰或集体表征支配的、某种社会秩序层面的现象。在1907年出版的《货币哲学》中，德国哲学家、社会学家格奥尔格·西美尔*分析了与社会互动和象征意义相关的经济体系，并表明事物的价值是变化的，而且是由社会建构的。[4] 社会学先驱马克斯·韦伯*于1904—1905年撰写的《新教伦理与资本主义精神》中分析了欧洲资本主义*的兴起过程，勾勒出宗教信仰、经济组织和个人行为三者之间的联系；[5] 资本主义是建立在工业和商业私有制基础上的社会经济模式，在当今西方世界（几乎遍及所有西方国家）中占据主导地位。

莫斯作品的独特之处在于关注了时间空间上跨度极大的古式社会，将研究重心从社会文化对经济行为的塑造转移到没有货币参与、以礼物交换为发生形式的交易行为上。《礼物》将社会现象的整体研究带向了一个不同的层面。

《礼物》于1923—1924年首次以法语发表在《社会学年鉴》上，直到30年后才被翻译成英文。《礼物》缺乏译本且只在学术期刊上发表，因此除了通晓多种欧洲语言的知识分子，很少有人能够接触到这篇文章。当时阅读了这篇文章的人可能对涂尔干的社会学思想及西美尔、韦伯的著作也非常熟悉。

虽然有多方限制，《礼物》刊发伊始便声名鹊起。该书的写作方式新颖，主题独特，在《社会学年鉴》上首刊后深寂多时，才由涂尔干的继承者之一重新编写，其素材来自包括 A. R. 拉德克利夫-布朗和布罗尼斯拉夫·马林诺夫斯基在内的多位民族志学者的作品，对英国结构功能主义学说的发展做出了贡献。

虽然一位研究新西兰土著文化的学者，人类学家雷蒙德·弗斯*，对莫斯阐释毛利人相关数据的方式提出异议，但这种对书中所用证据质量的顾虑并未妨碍该书产生广泛影响。[6] 几十年后，当学者开始重新思考前几代研究人员进行田野调查时所设定的假设前提时，这种顾虑再次显露。学者们对当时民族志材料的拼凑现象、研究人员的态度和能力进行了严厉批评，并重新评估了其研究结果的有效性。

局限性

莫斯认为，礼物交换是一种社会机制，以一系列与义务、名誉感和（至少在某些情况下的）与超自然力量有关的集体表征为基础，他的分析也经受住了时间的考验。虽然书中的一些想法已经过时，但该书的影响并未因其主题、理论研究方法或单一时空局限性而有所衰减。甚至在一些莫斯所不知道的游牧觅食 *（狩猎—采集）型社会中，也呈现出某些他发现的、存在于北美西北海岸的定居觅食者和乡村农耕者中的特征和动态变化情况，后者在 19 世纪末 20 世纪初成为全球民族志学者的研究对象。

《礼物》自出版以来并未遇到严峻挑战，即便是在社会达尔文主义（其基本观点是人类的技术、社会和智识会通过一系列固定的发展阶段而日趋完善，从而实现社会进步）、结构功能主义（关注社会建构方式和内部各部分协调方式的一种理论）连同比较分析方法论一起失去了青睐后，《礼物》仍然是许多学科的基础课本。莫斯只是有选择地接受了彼时流行一时的进化学说，并没有从根本上改变其分析的走向。他的比较方法完全立足于具体语境下对思想和实践的综合分析，而进化论者只是根据预定的分类方案拼凑社会事实，是一种对民族志研究的"机会主义"式应用。

莫斯和涂尔干的理论因所谓的"未能考虑个体因素和社会变化因素"而饱受诟病。然而，尽管他们关注的是集体表征和社会制度的问题，他们也思考了个体人格以及社会规范与个人信仰和行为之间的关系。他们提出了一种关于变化的理论，隐含在莫斯关于"礼物交换体系会随着政治经济组织的变化而变化"的分析中。[7]

《礼物》不仅仅涉及人类学和社会学，它也与语言学、经济学、历史学、哲学和政治学等人文学科和社会科学学科密切相关。该书一直以来为分析古往今来的人类行为和社会规范提供了一种基础范式，它是一本民族志肖像，如果没有它，人类早期社会的某些信息就会被遗忘殆尽了。

---

1. 马塞尔·莫斯：《礼物：古式社会中交换的形式与理由》，伦敦：劳特利奇出版社，1990 年，第 36、100—101 页。

2. 莫斯：《礼物》，第 65、112 页。

3. 玛丽·道格拉斯："前言：没有免费的礼物"，载马塞尔·莫斯著，《礼物》，伦敦：劳特利奇出版社，2000 年，第 xv 页。

4. 格奥尔格·西美尔：《货币哲学》，伦敦：劳特利奇出版社，1978 年。

5. 马克斯·韦伯：《新教伦理与资本主义精神：现代文化中宗教与经济社会生活的关系》，纽约：查尔斯·斯克里布纳出版社，1958 年。

6. 雷蒙德·弗斯：《新西兰毛利人的原始经济学》，伦敦：劳特利奇出版社，1929 年。

7. 道格拉斯："前言：没有免费的礼物"；赛斯·里柯克："马塞尔·莫斯的民族学理论"，《美国人类学家》第 56 卷，1954 年，第 58—71 页。

8 著作地位

要点 ⚏

- 马塞尔·莫斯的教学、写作和政治活动都围绕着一个中心展开：关注能够引导人际互动并促进社会团结的社会规范、共同信仰和法律结构。

- 《礼物》是莫斯研究方法的具体体现：它将早期的民族学比较（民族志材料的比较研究）与社会学理论相结合，并融入了对现代文明正反两面的思考。

- 《礼物》是莫斯最后一部以比较分析为主要研究方法的著作，是他最重要的学术贡献。他之后的作品在条件预设和研究方法上与《礼物》保持一致。

定位

人类学的奠基式人物克劳德·列维-斯特劳斯称《礼物》是马塞尔·莫斯的"杰作"和"最名副其实"的作品；[1]美国人类学家沃尔特·戈尔德施密特*称这是莫斯"最重要的独著作品"。[2]《礼物》象征着 19 世纪实证主义向 20 世纪社会人类学的过渡，前者是由法国哲学家奥古斯特·孔德建立的科学体系，即从数学学科到社会学等多个学科中抽离出其共有的基本原则和论证标准，以实现对各学科的整合统一，后者是在第一次世界大战前几年由涂尔干和他的同事们开创的。

纵观莫斯的职业生涯，他经常与他人合作研究，教授课业，终身学习，并将学术写作和政治写作结合起来。莫斯更专注于研究

"自己的材料"，而不是参与理论性的辩论或为其所看重的信条进行辩护。他打破了与其他学者之间的学科壁垒，建立了沟通桥梁，并通过坚持涂尔干实证主义强调的实证（可证实的）证据来避免冲突。法国人类学家莫里斯·林哈德*总结了莫斯的贡献："几乎没有哪本书或哪篇文章能够像《礼物》一样传播得如此之广，（该书）影响巨大。"[3]

除《礼物》之外，莫斯还对巫术、宗教、金钱、哀悼习俗、自杀行为、布尔什维主义*（政治运动，苏联*最初就是因这场运动建立）和暴力行为等有所研究。莫斯为期刊《社会学年鉴》撰写了若干短篇作品和书评，并编校了许多涂尔干及其他学者的未竟之作。此外，在人生的最后几年以及1950年去世后，莫斯在方法论、社会学和政治学领域的著作合集也陆续出版。[4]

第一次世界大战期间，莫斯的多位亲密合作伙伴都不幸罹难，加上两次世界大战之间的政治动荡，在《礼物》出版后，莫斯发表学术文章渐少，转而将精力移至政治激进主义和法国大学的制度发展上。他留下了几份关于布尔什维主义、祷告、民族和技术的未完成手稿。[5]

《礼物》中讨论的许多主题和实证证据都出现在莫斯早前撰写的文章中，如关于宗教、巫术和季节性生产活动的社会组织的文章。莫斯在政治上的激进立场使他的注意力集中在交换行为背后的法律机制和政治维度上。他虽然重视比较法，但仍然坚持，社会现象的研究必须放在社会整体语境背景下进行。总而言之，莫斯自身广泛的兴趣与其终生的追求是一致的，即从社会自身出发理解社会，从社会与社会的关系入手理解社会，从历史变化的角度入手理解社会。

> "通过对社会生活的具体观察，可以找到一些发现新鲜事实的方式，而我们只是刚刚有了一点模糊的认知而已。在我们看来，没有什么事情比研究整体社会事实更紧迫、更富有成效了。"
>
> —— 马塞尔·莫斯：《礼物：古式社会中交换的形式与理由》

整合

克劳德·列维-斯特劳斯认为，莫斯的思想走在了时代前列，是因为他认识到"人的内在精神世界和外在社会世界其实是一样的，是同一个世界"。[6]1926 年，莫斯在一份报告里阐述了文化信仰会对个人造成致命伤害的观点，反映出他非常重视社会—身体—心灵之间的纽带关系，认为这三者的结合可以形成一个新的整体。[7] 1934 年，莫斯在一篇名为《身体的技艺》的文章中探讨了文化信仰通过对身体机能的管理在孩童身上留下的印迹。[8] 同年，美国人类学家鲁思·本尼迪克特*也对美拉尼西亚、新墨西哥州和北美西北海岸的土著人族群进行了比较分析。在这两位学者的共同努力下，一门与文化、人格、精神能力、心理困扰相关的新兴学科逐渐发展起来。[9]

与此同时，在某些方面，莫斯仍然坚持自己的研究方式。在其职业生涯中，虽然他避免使用诸如"原始"或"劣等"之类的字眼，但他仍会根据社会的进化程度对社会形态进行分类。在 1938 年的一次演讲中，莫斯探讨了个体性的演变历程，演讲顺序与其在《礼物》中使用的民族志和历史资料顺序是一致的。[10]

莫斯的作品有一个一以贯之的主题：一方面是个体性，一方面经济行为受非经济体制、社会正义和社会凝聚力的制约，两者之间的关系究竟是怎样的？在《礼物》中，莫斯解释说，处于进化中期阶段的社会已经懂得如何将礼物关系制度化，以防止物资短缺和规避争斗，也消除了族群冲突带来的风险和不确定性。族群冲突是人类早期历史阶段的一个典型特征，那时个体人格的概念几乎不存在。[11]

社会进化的中期阶段出现了因个人原因而兴起的贸易形式，同时也出现了有助于团队领导人获取名誉、威望和商品的义务体系。在更先进的社会形态中，货币将交换关系与社会和道德环境脱离开来，使得个体性蓬勃发展，但古式社会物品交换的痕迹依旧存在，例如慈善捐赠、工人对工资无法与劳力等价的认识以及耗资无数的宴会等。莫斯认为应该将古代礼物交换中的互惠元素留存下来，以促进社会正义、经济增长和世界和平。在这一点上，他的学术旨趣和政治利益是不谋而合的。

意义

毫无疑问，《礼物》是莫斯最重要的学术遗产，是人类学专业学生的必读书目。它对其他一些比较分析案例有所启发，也促进了大量对互惠式交换关系的研究。虽然该书所采用的社会进化论的理论前提已经过时，比较研究的方法论自该书出版以来也遇到了严峻挑战，但莫斯对集体表征的见解以及对社会、经济、政治和宗教制度间相互关系的认识仍引人注目。

该书具有里程碑式意义，也是莫斯学识渊博、语言能力出众和学术严谨的证明。然而，仅凭该书不足以为他的声誉奠定基础。莫斯在政治上比较活跃，撰写并编纂了许多政治和学术著作，与多家学术机构合作，也担任过教师、演讲者。他与其他学者分享想法，合著了多部作品，也巩固了涂尔干对人文科学的影响。

虽然涂尔干的思想深刻影响了莫斯，莫斯也对此表示感激，但他仍坚持了自己的风格。与涂尔干不同，莫斯专注于他那个时代的政治斗争，并将其与他的学术工作联系了起来。不过，人们经常把他们放在一起加以批评，抨击他们过度强调虚无的社会事实而忽视个体，想当然地假设"集体表征可以紧密、稳定地契合社会制度"。然而，英国学者玛丽·道格拉斯则认为，涂尔干和莫斯都思考过个体思想在产生和维持集体表征方面发挥了怎样的作用，且并非对社会变化漠不关心。例如，《礼物》中的论证思路反映出一种经济交易方式从礼物交换转为契约贸易的社会变化理论。[12]

莫斯虽然以涂尔干的社会学传统为基础，但他是靠着自己独有的论点和学术发现声名远播的。《礼物》体现了莫斯的信念，即理解人类社会和个体行为的关键在于对记录着"整体社会事实"的、详尽可靠的语境化数据进行比较分析。

---

1. 赛斯·里柯克："马塞尔·莫斯的民族学理论"，《美国人类学家》第56卷，1954年，第65页；马赛尔·富尼耶：《马塞尔·莫斯传》，新泽西州普林斯顿：普林斯顿大学出版社，2005年，第1页。

2. 沃尔特·戈尔德施密特："对《礼物》的无题评论"，《美国人类学家》第57卷，1955年第6期，第1299页。

3. 富尼耶：《马塞尔·莫斯传》，第4页。

4. 马塞尔·莫斯：《民族志手册》，巴黎：帕约出版社，1947年；马塞尔·莫斯：《社会学与人类学》，巴黎：法国大学出版社，1950年。

5. 富尼耶：《马塞尔·莫斯传》；戈尔德施密特："对《礼物》的无题评论"；里柯

克："马塞尔·莫斯的民族学理论"。

6. 克劳德·列维-斯特劳斯：《马塞尔·莫斯作品介绍》，伦敦：劳特利奇 & 克感保罗出版社，1987 年，第 21 页。

7. 马塞尔·莫斯："集体暗示的死亡观念对个体的生理影响"，《心理学与病理心理学》第 23 卷，1926 年第 6 期，第 653—659 页。

8. 马塞尔·莫斯："身体的技艺"，《心理学与病理心理学》第 32 卷，1934 年第 3—4 期，第 271—293 页。

9. 列维-斯特劳斯：《马塞尔·莫斯作品介绍》，第 3—8、11—13 页。

10. 马塞尔·莫斯："人类精神的一个范畴"，《皇家人类学研究所学报》第 48 卷，1938 年第 2 期，第 263—281 页；里柯克："马塞尔·莫斯的民族学理论"，第 69—70 页。

11. 马塞尔·莫斯：《礼物：古式社会中交换的形式与理由》，伦敦：劳特利奇出版社，1990 年。

12. 玛丽·道格拉斯："前言：没有免费的礼物"，载马塞尔·莫斯著，《礼物》，伦敦：劳特利奇出版社，2000 年。

第三部分：学术影响

9 最初反响

要点 🔑

- 《礼物》之所以遭受批评，主要是因为其夸大了不同文化背景中某些概念和做法之间的连续性特征。评论者们还认为该书及其作者被进化论的理论框架束缚住了手脚，因循守旧，未能走向人类学和社会学的未来。

- 莫斯的支持者认为，莫斯在《礼物》中的分析在方法论上是合理的，从经验出发是准确的（即研究基于可证实的论据）。他们指出，莫斯其他的研究作品，如身心关联性、探索人类生存的社会和生物领域的相关性，也处于时代领先地位。

- 褒贬不一的主要原因是该书的英文译本 30 年后才出版。到了 20世纪 50 年代，社会达尔文主义和比较分析法在人类学研究中已经失宠，导致《礼物》在这两个方面受到抨击。

批评

《礼物》中引用了的大多数学者的观点，包括马林诺夫斯基和博厄斯在内的学者对该书的回应都是比较积极的。[1] 然而，人类学家雷蒙德·弗斯，一位新西兰土著文化专家，对其分析的原创性提出了质疑，并认为莫斯对毛利人的习俗和观念的解释有不当之处。[2]

莫斯去世后，1954 年，《礼物》英译本出版，旋即遭到那一代人类学家的批评，因为他们对寻求一般规律的研究思路、进化论的演进逻辑和比较分析方法论持谨慎态度。他们认为，莫斯之所以过分强调不同文化制度的相似性，忽略或淡化差异，可能是因为他缺乏田野调查经验。[3] 此外，莫斯不赞成英国人类学家 J. G. 弗雷泽在没有任何证据的情况下就认定图腾崇拜（将某物品神圣化并作为某一族群象征的行为）普遍存在，却将诸如"夸富宴"和"mana"（一种附属于物体的潜在超自然力量）等术语应用于其他缺乏本土对应概念的社会制度中，这也遭到了他们的诟病。[4] "夸富宴"是北美西北部土著居民中盛行的一种仪式性的宴会，其中包括赠送礼物的环节；它是参与者"炫富""炫名声"的一种手段，参与者甚至可以破坏物品以达到目的。

尽管莫斯探讨了如参与者妄自尊大、渴望贬低竞争对手等消极因素，评论者认为他还是低估了消极因素的力量，因为它们加大了"互惠式交换对增强社会凝聚力而言是必需品"这一大前提的复杂程度。沃尔特·戈尔德施密特提到，他在对莫斯笔下的社会进化中期阶段进行研究时，非常清楚地揭示了互惠式交换关系中存在着的贪婪、不道德和"冰冷的理性"。[5]

最后，当认识到简单社会形态下的各种制度不仅仅是复杂社会的前身时，人们就会质疑进化论用来调查和阐释人类社会活动的价值。这也导致许多评论家拒绝采纳莫斯得出的"把留存下来的互惠式交换形式加以拓展以促进现代社会的人际交流"的结论。

> "团队合作的工作理念，即坚信合作能够对抗孤陋，能够避免探索原创性时显露的自负情绪。以上应可概括我科研工作的特点，现在看来，这一点尤其明显。"
>
> —— 马塞尔·莫斯：《莫斯作品自述》

回应

一方面，如莫斯在 1938 年发表的一篇关于自主个体性演进历程的文章中所提到的那样，他是根据社会达尔文学说的理论框架来创作他的作品的。[6] 另一方面，尽管莫斯和涂尔干在 1901 年的文章里写道，社会事实一旦被科学地进行描述，就被简化成可供比较分析的数据，但莫斯一生都在宣扬语境化（考虑信息的社会和使用语境）是充分了解跨文化背景的必要基础。[7] 因此他并未轻易进行比较，正如他在《礼物》中指出的那样，凭空推测习俗是独立产生还是传播而来的做法"太容易也太危险了"。"就目前而言，能找到一个合适的主题，并阐述清其本质及广阔分布就应足够。至于书写这一论题的历史，就能者多劳吧。"[8]

为了使现代社会不那么冰冷无情、个人至上，莫斯将礼物交换的思想用于分析欧洲经济，但在 1930 年，莫斯却非常谨慎地看待从比较民族学中得出的与道德伦理相关的结论。当谈到将全球所有文化吸纳入单一的"普世"文化这一想法时，莫斯告诫，"不要将价值判断应用于这种趋势，因为它和'进步'一样，并不一定有好处或让人幸福。"[9] 莫斯无论在道义上还是体制上都坚定不移地支持 1937—1939 年在巴黎结识的社会学学院成员，特别是法国思想家乔治·巴塔耶 * 和罗杰·凯洛斯 *，但当他们把礼物中的观点用于分析现代社会的神圣之物，莫斯对他们的分析方法提出了反对意见。[10]

这些对《礼物》的批评在一定程度上解释了为什么该书是莫斯最后一本大部头的比较分析著作。《礼物》写成之后，他的注意力转向了其他话题，如从社会学视角探索心理现象和政治问题，但这些研究都没能促使莫斯对《礼物》的最初版本做出修订。

冲突与共识

莫斯作品的原创性受到了质疑——但是正如他 1930 年写的那样，他并不对原创性有太大兴趣。[11] 他更关心的是合作，是对具体

58

数据的分析和跨学科的思维。莫斯践行了自己所宣扬的互惠精神：善良，慷慨，并致力于与他人交流想法，分享资料。他本可以发表更多作品，最后《礼物》成为他为数不多的独著之一。

毋庸置疑的是，莫斯从人类学的视角，对经济系统如何嵌入包含政治、亲缘关系、宗教在内的更广泛的社会系统贡献了自己的想法。英国著名人类学家 E. E. 埃文斯-普里查德＊曾为 1954 年英译版《礼物》撰写导言，他在 1940 年的一部作品中将苏丹南部努尔人结婚时的财物往来现象描述为"家畜、妻子、儿童和男人等礼物循环中的一部分：每一种关系都可以具体化为一件礼物"。[12]

作为"法国民族志学之父"，莫斯对人类学研究的影响无可非议。[13] 虽然他个人没有实践经验，并且将田野调查看作一种短期的探索实践而非长期的调研工作，但其所教授的数据收集方法精确而全面。[14] 这一点在莫斯 1926—1939 年民族学研究所＊的演讲以及他的学生如社会学家亨利·莱维-布律尔＊的田野调查报告中都有所体现。[15]

莫斯的作品激励了几代学者在人类学领域砥砺前行，他们详细总结了互惠式交换的规律并将其当作研究相互关联的社会政治经济制度的切入点。[16] 在《亲缘关系的基本形式》中，按照克劳德·列维-斯特劳斯的描述，在一个强调责任共担和象征意义的社会网络中，男性、女性和儿童的所有权转移是一种礼物交换现象。换句话说，亲缘关系通过多重物品交换/交流系统的融合而产生。[17]

20 世纪 50 年代以后，学者们对假定客观性前提、追寻一般规律的做法展开了愈加严厉的批评，而这种做法是莫斯和涂尔干的其他追随者所拥护的。20 世纪 60、70 年代世界范围内发生的各种事件促使人们对知识来源进行重新思考，质疑早期那些没有受过严格训练、无意中带有文化偏见的田野调查者收集的数据是否有效。

1. 马赛尔·富尼耶：《马塞尔·莫斯传》，新泽西州普林斯顿：普林斯顿大学出版社，2005年，第244页。

2. 弗斯认为，尽管"hau"赋予礼物以生命力，但它并没有将任何送礼者的人格因素附加到礼物上。巴特却指出，来自印度的案例可以证明，为什么"hau"这一概念解释了各种社会形态中的礼物都承载着人格因素。弗雷德里克·巴特等：《人类学的四大传统：英国、德国、法国和美国人类学》，芝加哥：芝加哥出版社，2005年，第189页；雷蒙德·弗斯：《新西兰毛利人的原始经济学》，伦敦：劳特利奇出版社，1929年。

3. 赛斯·里柯克："马塞尔·莫斯的民族学理论"，《美国人类学家》第56卷，1954年，第59—60页；沃尔特·戈尔德施密特："对《礼物》的无题评论"，《美国人类学家》第57卷，1955年第6期，第1299页。

4. 里柯克："马塞尔·莫斯的民族学理论"，第63页。

5. 戈尔德施密特："对《礼物》的无题评论"，第1300页。

6. 里柯克："马塞尔·莫斯的民族学理论"，第70页。

7. 里柯克："马塞尔·莫斯的民族学理论"，第67页。

8. 马塞尔·莫斯：《礼物：古式社会中交换的形式》，伦敦：劳特利奇出版社，1990年，第98页。

9. 里柯克："马塞尔·莫斯的民族学理论"，第64页。

10. 富尼耶：《马塞尔·莫斯传》，第327页。

11. 马塞尔·莫斯："莫斯作品自述"，《法国社会学评论》第20卷，1979年第20—21期，第209页。

12. 玛丽·道格拉斯："前言：没有免费的礼物"，载马塞尔·莫斯著，《礼物》，伦敦：劳特利奇出版社，2000年，第xv页。

13. 乔治·孔多米纳："马塞尔·莫斯，法国民族志学之父"，《评论》第28卷，1972年297期，第118—139页。

14. 巴特等：《人类学的四大传统：英国、德国、法国和美国人类学》，第159页。

15. 马塞尔·莫斯：《民族志手册》，巴黎：帕约出版社，1947年。

16. 道格拉斯："前言：没有免费的礼物"，第xii—xiii页。

17. 克劳德·列维-斯特劳斯：《亲缘关系的基本形式》，波士顿：灯塔出版社，1969年；道格拉斯："前言：没有免费的礼物"，第xv页。

10 后续争议

要点 🔑

- 莫斯表明，一些无形的或无关紧要的交换行为实际上是人际关系和社会经济体系的核心。他的这一见解不断给研究简单和复杂社会形态中开放式互惠关系与社会凝聚力之间的联系带来新的启发。

- 《礼物》及其后续争议促使学界结合社会结构限制、比较视野下的经济政治制度、知识生产机制等方面对个人能动性*（行动的能力）展开研究。

- 《礼物》的影响是多方面的。其丰富的实证证据及对复杂现象的独到见解，堪称典范。然而该书建立在社会达尔文学说的假设基础上，未充分考虑该理论前提中的可变因素，因此其影响力局限在较早的年代，为后世研究指出了一些需要规避的风险。

应用与问题

　　莫斯最有影响力的作品《礼物》源自法国兴起的一股思潮，这股思潮旨在抵制 18、19 世纪英国哲学界兴起的、强调个体的功利主义理论。当时，莫斯与涂尔干以及其他学者一道，以《社会学年鉴》为平台，试图理解社会塑造个体思想和行为的方式。这些学者探讨了文化信仰与社会制度之间的相互作用，以及这种相互作用与社会凝聚力之间的关联。莫斯的贡献在于，他根据人在收到礼物一段时间后定会收到回馈这一现象描绘出了互惠式交换创造长久的、有约束力的社会关系的过程。

　　这一思潮很快与英国结构功能主义理论研究方法相融合，二者有着相同的基本假设，即社会各组成部分应共同运作，以维持稳定和平衡。以克劳德·列维-斯特劳斯为代表的法国结构主义*研究方法更专注于解释神话、宗教、仪式和故事中各元素的组织形式、相互关联状况以及它们对文化思想的表达方式。20 世纪 60、70 年代，所有形式的结构主义都受到了抨击，学者们质疑集体表征（社会成员的共同信仰和对事物的共同理解）的整合性力量过于死板，与社会个体所表达的思想相去甚远。[1]

于是学界的研究重点转移到个体和社会的分歧及文化动态性上。以维克多·特纳*以及克利福德·格尔茨*（他们分别以在非洲和印度尼西亚的工作而为人所熟知）为代表的象征人类学家或解释人类学家在具体案例中探索神话、宗教、仪式和符号的动态变化特征；他们研究了社会行动、社会结构的缺陷和倒置以及个体构建和表达意义的方式。法国社会学家皮埃尔·布尔迪厄关注的是权力及其不同的载体，如社会资本和符号资本，或如声誉及对知识的掌控等财富形式，同样可以像金融资产一样赋予所有者以权力。布尔迪厄重新引入了"惯习"*——社会和文化条件在个体身上的表现——这一经典概念，莫斯也在其 1934 年的文章《身体的技艺》[2]中探讨了童年阶段社会构建在个体身心留下的印记。生活经验、权力分配不公、语言文化这几者的内在关联为社会科学带来了新的研究焦点，即社会文化力量如何限制个体能动性（或者说，个体有认知并实现自己意愿的自由和资源）的问题。[3]

> "他的作品视野宏阔，想象充沛，虽然仍然建立在涂尔干精心建构的框架上，但放眼同时代，已鲜有匹敌。"
> —— 弗雷德里克·巴特*：《人类学的四大传统：英国、德国、法国和美国人类学》

思想流派

20 世纪上半叶，田野调查作品中出现了一些令人不安的细节，与此同时，结构主义和功能主义出现了阐释性和反思性的转向。根据克利福德·格尔茨的描述，马林诺夫斯基在日记中表露出与"当地人"在生理和心理上的隔阂，其用粗俗语言表达了对当地土著居民的冷漠和轻蔑。[4] 人类学家玛格丽特·米德*曾总结，三种社会形态下存在不同的性别系统，但她在新几内亚进行田野调查时脚踝受伤，对当地语言也不甚熟悉，这些问题影响了她的结论的可信度，而这一问题的根源似乎在于其个人生活和职业规划。[5] 列维-斯特劳斯同样参与过短暂的探险式田野考察，从他自己对民族志研究的描述中可以看出，他对当地土著语言也知之甚少。

民族志学者对此的回应方式则是将批判的眼光转向内部，开始反思自身的观点、社会地位及其背后更大的权力架构，在这种架构中，富人和受过良好教育的人比学者笔下的研究对象拥有更多的特权。一方面，人类学家自身扮演着研究工具的角色，会不可避免地对观察范围造成影响，使研究数据向对学界有利的一面倾斜。另一方面，这也使人们对以往民族志叙述的有效性以及包括莫斯在内的早期学者提出的比较分析主张产生了质疑。

莫斯的思想出现在现代社会学的成形期，因此对人文科学和社会科学产生了深远的影响。莫斯不仅仅是一位独立的思考者，也是一位信奉学术互惠的合作者。一个合适的说法是，他的思想并没有产生某个特定的思想流派，而是以各种低调的、偶尔间接的方式发挥作用。

当代研究

《礼物》一直带动着学术、文学、社会和政治领域的争鸣，对法国作家而言尤甚。莫斯（和涂尔干）证明了神圣物体（在精神层面有重要意义的物品）的属性与它们所被赋予的意义之间缺乏内在关联，这一理论与当时颇有影响力的瑞士语言学家费尔迪南·德·索绪尔*的语言教学思想不谋而合。他们的观点对列维-斯特劳斯开创的研究语言和神话的结构主义方法和精神分析学家雅克·拉康*倡导的在语言学、文学、心理学领域兴起的后结构主义*研究产生了深远的影响。[6]后结构主义理论排斥结构主义思想，尤其排斥结构主义宣扬的"通过分析可以得出任何客观事实"的想法。此外，许多学者的观点都直接源于莫斯的思想，哲学家保罗·利科*的"礼物经济"概念便是其中一例。[7]其他法国学者也从莫斯关于物品交换和人际关系的作品中汲取灵感，包括哲学家让-吕克·马里翁*、莫里斯·古德利尔*和雅克·德里达*（一位以"解构主义"方法分析符号和意义而著名的思想家）。[8]

《礼物》也对研究经济社会体系的社会学家和人类学家产生了持久的影响，如《礼物》促生了德国社会学家赫尔穆特·贝尔金*的《馈赠社会符号学》。[9]莫斯的思想也传到了美国学界，这在某种程度上要归功于匈牙利裔美国学者卡尔·波兰尼*及其对欧洲社会历史大作的介绍。美国学者乐于接受新思想，莫斯的观点也成为他们研究经济人类学的依据，他们对经济人类学的兴趣也与日俱增。[10]该领域近期的作品还有美国作家刘易斯·海德*对商业社会中创造力的经济意义和文化价值的研究，美国作家、法律学者理查德·海兰*整理的送礼明文规则的回顾以及美国历史学家哈里·李伯森*对工业时代礼物交换的描述。[11]

　　莫斯曾呼吁政治性写作和学术写作相结合，这一观点已经得到如艾伦·斯里福特*等对当代社会政策感兴趣的学者们的肯定。[12] 由法国思想家阿兰·卡耶*和杰拉尔德·贝尔图*于 1981 年发起的"社会科学中的反功利主义运动"（MAUSS）专注于经济危机、道德危机和环境危机等议题，其中，收入不稳定的问题，莫斯在《礼物》的结论中也有提及。[13] 卡耶一直担任杂志《莫斯评论》的编辑。杂志题目中有**"社会科学中的反功利主义运动"**的首字母缩写，这是为了纪念莫斯对法国社会学的深远影响。

1. 玛丽·道格拉斯："前言：没有免费的礼物"，载马塞尔·莫斯著，《礼物》，伦敦：劳特利奇出版社，第 2000 年；赛斯·里柯克："马塞尔·莫斯的民族学理论"，《美国人类学家》第 56 卷，1954 年，第 58—71 页。

2. 马塞尔·莫斯："身体的技艺"，《心理学：正常与病理》第 32 卷，1934 年第 3—4 期，第 271—293 页。

3. 皮埃尔·布尔迪厄：《实践理论概述》，剑桥：剑桥大学出版社，1977 年；克利福德·格尔茨："从本土的角度来看"，载克利福德·格尔茨著，《地方知识》，纽约：基础读物出版社，1983 年，第 54—70 页；维克多·特纳：《戏剧、田野与隐喻：人类社会的象征性行为》，纽约州伊萨卡：康奈尔大学出版社，1974 年；维克多·特纳：《仪式过程：结构与反结构》，芝加哥：阿尔丁出版社，1969 年。

4. 格尔茨："从本土的角度来看"，第 54—55 页。

5. 莉兹·M. 多布林和艾拉·巴世科："'阿拉佩什的战争'：雷奥·福群对玛格丽特·米德性别与气质一书的含蓄批评"，《美国人类学家》第 112 卷，2010 年第 3 期，第 370—383 页；玛格丽特·米德：《三个原始部落的性别与气质》，纽约：威廉莫洛出版社，1935 年。

6. 费尔迪南·德·索绪尔：《普通语言学教程》，纽约：麦格劳-希尔出版社，
   1959 年。

7. 保罗·利科：《记忆、历史、遗忘》，芝加哥：芝加哥大学出版社，2004 年。

8. 让-吕克·马里翁：《被给予的存在：关于被给予性的现象学研究》，加利福尼
   亚州帕罗奥多：斯坦福大学出版社，2002 年；莫里斯·古德利尔：《礼物之
   谜》，巴黎：法亚尔出版社，1996 年；雅克·德里达：《赠予死亡》，芝加哥：
   芝加哥大学出版社，2007 年；雅克·德里达：《被赠予的时间：伪造的钱币》，
   芝加哥：芝加哥大学出版社，1992 年。

9. 赫尔穆特·贝尔金：《馈赠的社会符号学》，伦敦：圣哲出版社，1999 年。

10. 里柯克："马塞尔·莫斯的民族学理论"，第 65 页；卡尔·波兰尼：《大转型：
    我们时代的政治和经济起源》，纽约：法勒和菜因哈特出版社，1944 年。

11. 刘易斯·海德：《礼物：创新精神如何改变世界》，纽约：古典书局，2008 年；
    理查德·海兰：《礼物：比较法研究》，牛津：牛津大学出版社，2009 年；哈
    里·李伯森：《礼物的回归：全球观念下的欧洲史》，纽约：剑桥大学出版社，
    2011 年。

12. 艾伦·斯里福特编：《礼物的逻辑：慷慨背后的伦理学分析》，伦敦：劳特利奇
    出版社，1997 年。

13. 阿兰·卡耶：《礼物人类学：人类学的第三种范式》，巴黎：德克莱和德·布劳
    威尔出版社，2000 年。

11 当代印迹

要点 🔑

- 《礼物》仍然是人类学教学的基础课本。该书现今仍然影响着学界对互惠式交换的解读，影响着互惠式交换与社会凝聚力、和平和幸福生活之间的关系。

- 目前学界仍在研究礼物交换和商业交易对社会和个人的政治和经济意义，《礼物》一书至今仍然受用。

- 如今，各学者填补了不同文化间经济交换方面的知识空白，为个人和社会在加强社会关系、改善生活、避免人际冲突和国际冲突方面提供了思路。

地位

　　莫斯在创作《礼物》时，西方学者还生活在等级社会中，认为统治者和社会不平等现象的存在是理所当然的。随后，社会学家、哲学家皮埃尔·布尔迪厄对权力、冲突和内部分化进行了批判性的分析。今天，莫斯作品中的盲区已被其他学者填补，为读者解读他的结论、理解他的结论对经济政策和人际关系的影响开辟了新的道路。

　　莫斯无意中使用的某种概念框架带有他自身的特色，如他的阶级、性别以及他所在的历史阶段，这一框架在莫斯对性别的考量中尤为明显，他认为女性是贸易商品，而男性通常为决策者。[1]这种观点极不恰当，美国人类学家安妮特·韦娜*关于特罗布里恩群岛的分析以及英国人类学家玛丽莲·斯特拉森*对美拉尼西亚的分析已经反驳了这一点。[2] 早期人类学家观念中的这一盲区足以证明他们无意识中的某些假设使他们自己的观念扭曲，对性别相互依存的事实、母系亲缘关系（女方一脉的家庭关系）的深远影响视而不见。

莫斯对等级制度全盘接受，绝无批判。这一点可见于其作品中关于象征体系和制度体系的代际传递、历代因互惠交换而造成的社会不公现象的描述。他并未从那些人们居无定所、以狩猎或觅食为生的无阶级、无领袖、性别平等的社会形态中获得启发，因为这种社会形态在几十年后才为人所知。[3] 20 世纪 70 年代以来，人类学家研究了大约 50 个这样的族群，它们才是互惠交换真正的拥护者。它们与《礼物》中描述的以美国西北海岸某些族群为代表的定居觅食型社会不同，后者并不多见，且存在着领导者、社会等级以及长期的财富储备等现象。

觅食型社会践行高度规则化的互惠形式，但也非常重视个体自主性（个体行事能力），这对莫斯和涂尔干提出的"个体性只能在复杂的现代社会中得到充分体现"的假设是一项挑战。这一挑战并未让莫斯的作品完全退出历史舞台。相反，书中关于互惠和再分配的观点的修正使得该书的影响扩展至对当前政治、经济及人际关系等诸多议题的讨论。

> "我们不应该将对物质的渴望视作理所当然。正如马塞尔·莫斯说的那样，这种渴望与其说是背后支配我们的先天条件，倒不如说是摆在我们面前供选择的一种道德价值观。因此，它与其说是必然的，倒不如说是后天创造出来的。"
>
> —— 马歇尔·萨林斯 *:《向修昔底德致歉：将历史理解为文化，反之亦然》

互动

马歇尔·萨林斯所描绘的"富裕的原始社会"指的是无正式领袖的流动的觅食型社会，由生活在一起的个人和家庭小团体组成。[4]在这类社会中，人们平常不储存食物，财产若不易携带也不会积攒。分享食物也有严格精细的规则，特别是一些珍贵食物。通常，女性和男性上交的食物量相等。与种植者相比，觅食者工作时间更少，健康状况更好。

与莫斯笔下的部落成员相似，觅食者受益于群体之间的互惠行为，因为这种互惠行为可以防止物资匮乏，阻止暴力冲突。在群体中，互惠行为是一种制衡机制，可以使人们保持谦逊，防止嫉妒情绪的滋长。傲慢情绪会威胁个体自主性的发挥，更有可能导致暴力事件。若社会成员不去工作或无法满足家庭需求，无法履行其他相类似的义务，则会受到其他社会成员的谴责。

觅食型社会向西方关于史前史和人性的假设提出了挑战。贪婪、等级观念、男性主导一切的想法、领地意识、侵略意识和个人利益至上的观点，这些被视为人类自身所固有的特征，在觅食型社会的佐证下，在短暂的生命、无尽的穷困和屈从于暴君这样残酷的背景下，逊色不少。而这些关于人性的假设正是各类功利主义哲学（概括来说，是指使实用性等同于自身价值的哲学流派）的核心思想，包括支撑当今资本主义制度的自由市场经济学和现今的社会达尔文主义[5]（指用进化论解释不同的个体或群体在生理上的劣势或优越性为何会带来不同的特征和命运）。现今的社会达尔文主义还吸收了遗传学的思想。

人类学家通过研究部落间战争、联姻和其他交换行为间的联系，证实了莫斯关于互惠行为有助于减少冲突的观点。[6]同样，一些非正式的法律制度也可以证明这一观点，这些制度将发生争执的人聚集在一处，由家族成员一起参与调解。[7]跨文化背景下的交换行为有助于建立起长久的关系，防止国际冲突。但另一方面，正如莫斯所说的那样，像赈灾和国际援助等无法进行回馈的礼物只会通过牺牲获赠者的利益来增强赠送者的地位和权力。[8]

持续争议

莫斯从未试图调和社会不公和社会凝聚力 * 之间的矛盾。觅食型社会表明，不平等不是事物的本质，这也给予了探索社会中权力分配和不和谐现象的人类学家以有力支持。正如我们所看到的那样，互惠交换因物质商品缺乏积累而产生，交换双方必须彼此公平，因而阻止了阶级的产生。性别平等源于男女双方互补或各自独立的食物采集方式。然而，匈牙利裔美国人类学家欧内斯廷·弗里德尔 * 表示，当男性控制着某种稀有的、难以预知的资源的分配，如大型动物的肉的分配，公平性偶尔也会降低。控制具有交换价值的事物则会产生不平等现象。[9]这种模式说明了互惠式交换是如何对同一社群中的不同性别群体造成了影响。它还表明，无论何种情况下，当单一的性别群体控制着名誉和恩惠等宝贵资源，更高层次的不平等就会出现。

弗里德尔的分析与莫斯的假设相同，即所有的互惠式交换都具有社会、经济和政治意义。交换过程可能并没有货币参与，或者在有货币流通的社会中，相同的资源既可用于维护家庭利益（"使用价值"），也可用于家庭成员之外以培养潜在的、富有成效的社会关系（"交换价值"）。正如莫斯所表明的那样，所有社会形态中，互惠交易和交易性买卖都是共存的。

　　这意味着，与不公平的社会分配体系相比，平等的交换系统更有可能促进社会成员的团结，因为平等的交换系统可以在维持社会凝聚力的同时保有个体的自主性。从这个角度看，这与莫斯更看重良善社会的想法并不是相斥的。社会成员具有个体性，有工作的义务和捍卫自身利益（从自我到社会）的权利，并不与回馈个人的社会职能（通过教育、收入保障、公平的粮价和房价、公道的佣金、健康及生活保障进行回馈）相排斥。关键是对个人主义要有更全面的看法，若想践行莫斯提出的抵制贪婪、囤积和唯利是图的相关措施，必须改变基于个人功利主义的法律框架。当今学界正在研究的社会的高度融合与更好的经济、健康、教育和犯罪状况之间的关系，也进一步支持了莫斯提出的构想。[10]

1. 马塞尔·莫斯：《礼物：古式社会中交换的形式与理由》，伦敦：劳特利奇出版社，1990 年，第 5—6 页。

2. 玛丽莲·斯特拉森：《礼物的性别：女性问题和美拉尼西亚的社会问题》，伯克利：加州大学出版社，1988 年；安妮特·韦娜：《有价值的女人，有名望的男人：特罗布里恩群岛交换行为新解》，奥斯汀：得克萨斯大学出版社，1976 年。

3. 莫斯提到的中非"俾格米人"住在村庄附近的森林里，早于其他大多数觅食族群为传教士和其他外国人所知晓。

4. 马歇尔·萨林斯：《石器时代的经济学》，纽约：阿尔定德古意特出版社，1972 年，第 1 页。

5. 马歇尔·萨林斯：《人性的西方幻象：对西方等级制度、平等主义及无政府主义崇拜历史的反思，以及对其他人类状况概念的比较》，芝加哥：仙人掌出版社，2008 年。

6. 道格拉斯·P. 弗赖伊：《人类追求和平的潜力：人类学向战争和暴力的假设提出的挑战》，纽约：牛津大学出版社，2006 年。

7. 弗赖伊：《人类追求和平的潜力》。

8. 李·克朗克："附加条款"，《科学杂志》第 29 卷，1988 年第 3 期，第 2—4 页。

9. 欧内斯廷·弗里德尔："社会与性别角色"，《人性》第 1 卷，1978 年，第 8—75 页。

10. 马塞尔·莫斯：《礼物》，第 68—89 页；理查德·威尔金森和凯特·皮克特：《社会不平等：为何国家越富裕，社会问题越多》，纽约：布鲁姆斯伯里出版社，2009 年。

12 未来展望

要点 ⚷━

- 《礼物》是一部影响巨大的著作，它分析了礼物的流通循环和社会关系之间的联系，参与了思想史的发展演变，并能随时代变化不断创新。

- 莫斯关于互惠式礼物交换中的神圣或巫术元素的研究对未来社会可能也会有影响。

- 莫斯对赠送和接受礼物的分析（包括礼物中神秘属性的转移），与身体器官交易、社交媒体时代的社会关系以及当前时代的其他问题研究息息相关。

潜力

马塞尔·莫斯的《礼物》探讨了礼物交换中的神圣元素，丰富了进一步调研的可能性。莫斯指出，在古式社会，宗教献祭是人们与神灵保持互惠关系的一种手段。[1] 献祭方式包括向神灵进献礼物以及对穷人布施以酬谢过往神灵对自己的恩惠，并期待借此不断获取利益。在未来，《礼物》可能影响到的领域之一就是研究宗教情感在多大程度上促进了商业化社会形态中的慈善捐赠。他的建议是社会应鼓励富人将自己视为财富（通过某种自然力量而获得）的临时保管者，并作为其他人的金融托管者履行相应的职责。这一观点在当代关于税法、慈善捐赠、教育及社会服务的思辨讨论中占有一席之地。莫斯指出，这些讨论需要解决的是作为献祭任务的馈赠与贡品循环维系社会体系这一事实之间的矛盾。

拓展莫斯思想的另一种方式是探索巫术在现代社会中扮演的角色。有人指出，西方社会仍认为祖先喜爱的某种食物或者从远方引流而来的泉水中具有某种超自然的力量。[2] 一些流行的概念如"**羯磨**"（佛教和印度教的信条，一个人累积的功德决定了他此生或来世的命运）、"善有善报"（积极的行为会成为"善"的循环中的一环）都表明超自然力量能够作用于个体生活，即人们以神秘的方式互相关联，一个人每天的活动都会对未来产生影响。尽管经济学和政治学领域出现了向功利主义回归（回归到高度务实的推测和政策中，认为效用的重要性高于其他如伦理等无法衡量的因素）的趋势，科学学科日益受到尊重，但留存于当代文化中的神圣及巫术元素仍为拓展莫斯的思想提供了巨大的分析空间。

> 　　"人们总是对人体器官进行精心的隐喻再加工以压制（伦理上的）不和谐声音。最常见也最明显的例子是给器官贴上'生命之馈赠'的标签，这样就迅速模糊了（捐献行为）本质上是经济活动的事实，并将其神秘化。"
>
> 　　　　—— 莱斯利·夏普＊："商品化的亲缘关系：死亡、哀悼以及美国关于器官捐献者遗体的不同主张"

未来方向

　　《礼物》指出，纯粹出于慷慨而不期待回馈的送礼行为是不合乎逻辑的，人们总会期待各种各样非物质的回馈，如声望或自我满足等。以献血为例，英国社会政策学创始人理查德·蒂特马斯＊承认捐赠者可以通过献血获得社会认可，也能够感受到他们有朝一日可能也需要输血的需求，但他坚持献血者是为了社会团结而献出血液，是一种有意识的道德行为。[3] 因此，为了鼓励捐赠，赠送礼物一定不能为金钱交易所腐蚀。

然而，医学人类学家玛格丽特·洛克*认为，之所以会产生上述观点，是因为市场经济与互惠交换经历了人为的不必要的区分。她指出，传统经济融入市场经济时，互惠式礼物交换系统并未消失，而是成为一套与现有机制平行或混合的制度。[4]同样，在捐赠行业，生物性的移植以经济交易为基础，而在未被认可的互惠式交换体系中，礼物承担着社会性义务，这两者是可以共存的。

洛克解释说，器官移植行业有意对人体器官进行"恋物崇拜"（德国经济学家、政治哲学家卡尔·马克思*使用的术语）：人体器官在马克思称之为"商品客体化"的过程中成为具有非凡价值的物体，从而掩盖了生产和消费中的剥削关系。洛克认为，从原始意义上来说，器官也是被物化的，被赋予了个性和巫力，这一点莫斯也是认同的："单独的身体部位仍是具有生命力的，甚至是有个性的……器官被取得并移植后，若接受者认为这一拯救生命的器官具有泛灵论*的特性，那么他就会被严厉责难，甚至被认为精神异常。"[5]

为避开伦理争端，医务人员煞费苦心将捐献器官这种礼物定义为一个与任何生理痛苦或者公司利益都不相关的、可以无偿获得的物体。在这种情况下，器官仅仅是冰冷的商品（简而言之，有用的物品），与人无关，也不能产生义务——但捐助者和接受者家庭也会通过其他方式了解实情，双方会如一般的礼物交换一样建立起关系。[6]

小结

莫斯表明，礼物使个人、家庭、社会和国家永久地联系在一起，三者彼此间形成债务关系，不断循环。礼物是鲜活的，有其人格和精神价值，它们要求获赠者以某种方式回馈赠送者。这些想法与当代社会高度相关，有助于从经济和道德层面分析自愿性的生物体移植行为，如越来越多的 DNA（一种用于为基因信息编码并将其传递给后代的生物体）移植。[7]莫斯的观点解释了为谋求业务发展或满足个人需求而自愿捐赠礼金的赠礼方式，如众筹（个人捐赠，特别是通过在线网络社区为小企业筹集资金），也阐明了通过软件开源、内容免费及开设以技术和创意交流为节点的网站等方式自愿提供知识财富的赠礼方式。[8]

此外，《礼物》也指出纯商业交易如何错失了提高社会凝聚力的机会。礼物的循环流通延滞了当下人际关系的发展；这虽然违背了许多人的意愿，但却带来了实际的好处。研究证实，社会凝聚力的提高有助于社会成员改善身心健康，加强成员相互间义务的落实程度。莫斯希望探知个体是如何在嵌入大众社会的同时保持了自主性，即个人经济行为是如何受到了非经济机制的约束。这个问题已经通过对俱乐部和志愿者协会的研究得到了解决。在大型工业化社会的各个群体中，凝聚力源于成员间相互间履行义务，并主动避免等级分化的做法，这种做法对个人也是有利的。[9]

莫斯的思想影响了几代读者。他告诉我们，礼物既富有表现力又具有工具性。人与人之间的交换行为——不论是个体还是群体——都处于更加宏观的、体现着社会不公的规则权力体系中。无论是金钱、物质产品还是无形之物，物品转移都带有文化构建的象征价值和意义，使社会关系得到巩固。

1. 马塞尔·莫斯和亨利·于贝尔:《献祭的性质与功能》,伦敦:劳特利奇出版社,1964 年。

2. 马歇尔·萨林斯:《人性的西方幻象:对西方悠久历史中等级制度、平等思想及无政府主义崇拜的反思,以及对其他人类状况概念的比较》,芝加哥:仙人掌出版社,2008 年。

3. 理查德·蒂特马斯:《礼物关系:从人类血液到社会政策》,纽约:新兴出版社,1997 年。

4. 玛格丽特·洛克:《二度死亡:器官移植与重新发明死亡》,伯克利:加州大学出版社,2001 年,第 316 页。

5. 洛克:《二度死亡》,第 320 页。

6. 莱斯利·P.夏普:"商品化的亲缘关系:死亡、哀悼以及美国关于器官捐献者遗体的不同主张",《美国人类学家》第 103 卷,2001 年第 1 期,第 112—133 页。

7. 迪帕·雷迪:"实现共同利益的上好礼物:遗传学研究市场中的血液和生物伦理",《文化人类学》22 卷,2007 年第 3 期,第 429—472 页。

8. 克里斯多夫·凯尔蒂:《两比特:自由软件的文化意义》,北卡罗来纳州达勒姆:杜克大学出版社,2008 年。

9. 理查德·威尔金森和凯特·皮克特:《社会不平等:为何国家越富裕,社会问题越多》,纽约:布鲁姆斯伯里出版社,2009 年。

术语表

1. **类同性**："物以类聚"的原理，"感应巫术"的基础，通过"感应巫术"的仪式如祈雨舞模仿所需之物。

2. **能动性**：认知并实现自我意愿所必需的自由和资源。

3. **古欧亚大陆**：包括古希腊、古罗马、古印度和中东地区在内的文明古国。

4. **泛灵论**：万物有灵。

5. **《社会学年鉴》**：法国社会学家涂尔干于1898年创办此期刊，用于发表他及其学生的社会学研究成果。社会学是一门由涂尔干创立的新兴学科。

6. **人类学**：研究人类生物学史、文化史及其当前变化的学科。

7. **反犹主义**：针对犹太人或犹太教的仇恨、偏见和歧视。

8. **古式社会**：莫斯对当代土著社会以及代表社会进化中期阶段的古代文明的称谓。

9. **以物易物**：现场交换不同的物品，可能涉及讨价还价。

10. **布尔什维主义**：俄国社会民主工人党1903—1917年发起的运动，最终俄工党夺取政权建立共产党政府，并在五年内建立了苏联。

11. **资本主义**：建立在工商业私有制基础上的社会经济模式，现如今在西方世界（几乎遍及所有西方国家）占据主导地位。

12. **氏族**：通过血缘或婚姻关系建立起来、拥有共同祖先的亲族。

13. **集体表征**：社会成员的共同信仰和对事物的共同理解。

14. **集体主义**：一种哲学流派，涉及伦理、政治和社会多个领域，关注群体特征，反对个人主义。

15. **比较分析**：通过比较不同的社会体系、人工制品或特征对社会或群体进行的对比研究。

16. **接触**：原始巫术中的一条原则，认为源于人体产物之类的物品中永久存在着某种神秘力量，人们接触到这些物品便可以操纵这种力量。

17. **合作社运动**：19 世纪欧洲为应对工业革命和生产机械化带来的社会动荡和失业危机而推广的一种经济制度。

18. **文化**：群体内成员认同的一系列动态的、不受限制的信仰、行为预期、价值观、创造形式和知识。

19. **通货**：从贝壳、农产品到黄金、纸币在内的任何交换媒介。

20. **实证方法**：认为所有知识都应该通过实证方式（通过实验和观察来收集事实真相）获得。

21. **爱斯基摩人**：居住于北美洲的北极海岸、格陵兰岛和西伯利亚的北极地区土著民族；也称为因纽特人。

22. **民族志**：既指通过学习族群当地语言、长期沉浸于该语言环境等方式，对一个族群展开的系统研究；也指对田野调查数据的书面分析。

23. **民族学**：关于民族志数据分析和文化异同比较的学科。

24. **觅食**：一种以食物收集而非农耕或畜牧为主的生活方式；也称为狩猎和采集。

25. **法国工人党**：法国社会主义政党，于 1880 年成立，1905 年并入法国社会党。

26. **惯习**：在古代，指影响个人身体状况和脆弱程度的体质因素与环境因素。在当前的学术语境中，该概念侧重于社会和文化条件在个体身上的表现。

27. **Hau**：毛利人认为的某一类礼物拥有的、使人们传递自身并使自身归于原位的力量。

28. **历史特殊论**：与弗朗兹·博厄斯相关的人类学理论动向，强调记录历史背景下族群生活细节的重要性，关注个别社会的独特性。

29. **整体**：强调整体的重要性，各组成部分不可分割。

30. **土著**：某地的原始居民；通常用于指涉因政府行为或外来移民迁入定居而被边缘化的、无家可归的人。

31. **民族学研究所**：由罗·里韦、马塞尔·莫斯和吕西安·莱维-布吕尔共同创办的法国民族学研究所。

32. **制度**：传统的社会关系或活动，如退休或婚姻；也可指正式的法人实体，如学校或法院等。

33. **亲缘关系**：通过生子、婚姻、洗礼、收养等可以定义亲属关系的社会手段而产生的人际关联。

34. **库拉**：在特罗布里恩群岛之间进行的臂章和项圈的循环性、礼节性的交换行为。

35. **自由主义**：一种基于个体自主性的政治哲学思想，强调自由市场经济和不受个人自由意志干涉的法治秩序。

36. **Mana**：波利尼西亚人和美拉尼西亚地区人认为，"mana"是一种无处不在的超自然力量，遍及宇宙，依附于物体，并通过某些人群的优势和力量展现出来。

37. **毛利人**：新西兰土著居民。

38. **市场经济**：基于商品既定价值的经济交易模式，但不仅仅指发生在实体市场中的交换行为。

39. **美拉尼西亚**：西南太平洋中群岛，介于赤道与澳大利亚东北部之间，包括所罗门群岛、新喀里多尼亚和巴布亚新几内亚。

40. **人格**：特定文化和社会背景下个体的状态，在西方思想中"人"是社会的个体，而"自我人格"特指个体的内心世界。

41. **波利尼西亚**：散布于中南太平洋、介于新西兰、夏威夷和复活岛之间的多个岛屿。

42. **后结构主义**：反对结构主义二元论的一系列理论路径和方法论，强调概念范畴及其意义的易变性和变化。

43. **夸富宴**：北美西北部土著居民中盛行的一种仪式性的盛宴，其中包括赠送礼物的环节；它是参与者通过增加礼物数量甚至毁坏财物的方法来"炫富""炫名声"的一种手段。

44. **俾格米人**：中非森林地区的土著民族。

45. **理性**：经济学中，推理论证的一个特性，人们通过权衡边际成本和收益，实现效用最大化。

46. **互惠**：个人或群体之间有形、无形礼物和服务的循环交换。

47. **革命社会主义工人党**：1890—1901 年法国温和的改革派政党，宗旨是促进教育和劳动保障。

48. **神圣**：范畴或形容词，指值得进行宗教崇拜的思想、仪式和物体。

49. **季节性**：人们的行为模式根据季节变化而变化。

50. **社会进化阶段论**：认为人类的技术、社会发展和智识水平会通过一系列固定的发展阶段而日趋完整；进化速度的差异解释了为何会同时存在不同的发达社会形态。

51. **社会主义**：一种政治制度，其中生产资料（工商业所需的工具和资源）为社会成员所共有。

52. **社会学**：研究社会行为、社会制度以及人类社会起源和组织方式的一门学科。

53. **凝聚力**：人们感到的彼此关联的程度。

54. **苏联**：全称苏维埃社会主义共和国联盟，1917 年俄国十月革命后崛起的欧亚大国（1922—1991 年），包括俄罗斯以及东欧、波罗的海、黑海、中亚地区的 14 个卫星国家。

55. **结构功能主义**：与布罗尼斯拉夫·马林诺夫斯基与 A. R. 拉德克利夫–布朗相关的人类学及社会学理论方法，侧重于社会建构和社会的内部整合方式。

56. **结构主义**：一种分析社会、文本或语言形式的方法，会将分析对象的基本组成部分放入二元对立体系中考虑；人类学家克劳德·列维–斯特劳斯的思想与这一方法有关。

57. **图腾**：一个融入了神圣力量的中性物体；某一族群的象征。

58. **贸易**：以既定价值标准为依据的不同物品的正式交换。

59. **部落**：以亲缘关系为政治组织核心的一类社会形态。

60. **功利主义**：事物价值由其有用性决定的观念；18、19 世纪的英国哲学传统，代表人物为杰里米·边沁和约翰·斯图亚特·穆勒，其在伦理意义上的目的是帮助集体实现效用最大化，是某个行为所产生的所有幸福感的总和，减去参与此行为的所有人的痛苦（简明扼要地说，即让最多的人收获最大的利益）。

61. **效用**：在经济学中，消费者所购商品和服务在生理和 / 或心理层面的有用性。

62. **第一次世界大战**：1914 年至 1918 年间爆发的战争，期间奥匈帝国、德国、土耳其和保加利亚被英国、法国、意大利、俄罗斯、日本、美国和其他盟国击败。

63. **第二次世界大战**：1939 年至 1945 年间爆发的全球性冲突，涉及多个大国和许多其他国家。同盟国（美国、英国、法国、苏联等）和轴心国（德国、意大利、日本等）之间的斗争，在道德层面上，被视为一场自由与暴政之间的重要斗争。

人名表

1. 弗雷德里克·巴特（1928 年生），挪威人类学家，具有广泛的田野调查工作经验。他以政治和经济组织、种族以及智识方面的著作而闻名。

2. 乔治·巴塔耶（1897—1962），法国作家、哲学家，他的作品涵盖许多个人文学科，还包括一些离经叛道小说和短篇故事。

3. 亨利·伯夏（1878—1914），法国社会学家，涂尔干和莫斯的同事。他在西伯利亚东北海岸的一个离岛上探险时因曝晒和饥饿不幸罹难。

4. 鲁思·本尼迪克特（1887—1948），美国人类学家，对民俗、艺术、语言和个性领域感兴趣。她在比较文化和文化述行性方面的研究较为出名。

5. 杰里米·边沁（1748—1832），英国法学家、哲学家，功利主义哲学的创始人。

6. 赫尔穆特·贝尔金（1952 年生），德国社会学家，对经济人类学、城市人类学、社会理论和文化身份研究感兴趣。

7. 杰拉尔德·贝尔图（1935 年生），瑞士社会学家、经济学家，与阿兰·卡耶一同发起社会科学中的反功利主义运动。

8. 莫里斯·布洛赫（1939 年生），英国人类学家，曾在马达加斯加进行田野调查。他是一名杰出的学者，并从 1983 年起至今在伦敦经济学院任教授。

9. 弗朗兹·博厄斯（1858—1942），德裔美国人类学家，美国人类学历史特殊论学派创始人，研究美国西北海岸的土著居民生活。他被认为是"美国人类学之父"。

10. 皮埃尔·布尔迪厄（1930—2002），法国社会学家、哲学家、人类学家，学术兴趣点是反思性、语言、社会资源以及权力的动态性。

他以对某些概念如惯习、社会资本、象征资本和文化资本的阐释而闻名。

11. **阿兰·卡耶**（1944年生），法国社会学家、经济学家，"社会科学中的反功利主义运动"的发起人之一，杂志《莫斯评论》的编辑，在《礼物》的启发下撰写了不少著作。

12. **罗杰·凯洛斯**（1913—1978），法国作家、社会学家和政治哲学家。他因在神圣之物、游戏、戏剧以及拉丁美洲文学方面的研究而闻名。

13. **乔治·孔多米纳**（1921—2011），法国人类学家，对越南进行过研究，师从丹尼丝·波尔姆、马塞尔·格里奥列和莫里斯·林哈德。

14. **查尔斯·达尔文**（1809—1882），英国博物学家，他因提出进化论、尤其是自然选择理论（认为所有动物有着共同的祖先）而声名远播。

15. **雅克·德里达**（1930—2004），法国社会学家，出生于阿尔及利亚，是解构主义符号分析法的先驱。

16. **乔治·德弗罗**（1908—1985），匈牙利裔法国人类学家、精神分析师，克劳德·列维-斯特劳斯的亲密伙伴。他是公认的民族精神病学之父。

17. **玛丽·道格拉斯**（1921—2007），英国社会人类学家，对象征主义、比较宗教、经济和环境人类学感兴趣。她因其神圣范畴的结构主义分析著作《洁净与危险》（1966）而闻名。

18. **艾尔弗雷德·德雷福斯**（1859—1935），法国炮兵军官，信奉犹太教，因叛国罪而被秘密军事法庭判处流放并终身监禁。他因"德雷福斯案件"而在1899年得到总统赦免。1906年，德雷福斯由军方正式平反，重返军队服役。

19. **埃米尔·涂尔干**（1858—1917），法国社会科学家，被视为社会学的学科创立者。涂尔干的社会学融合了孔德的实证主义社会学，以人文主义的视角关注社会成员的共同信仰和价值观。他因异化、自杀和社会学研究法方面的著作而闻名。

20. 艾尔弗雷德·维克托·埃斯皮纳斯（1844—1922），法国哲学家，他的文章多与政治哲学，思想文化史和人类思想演变相关。

21. E. E. 埃文斯·普里查德（1902—1973），英国社会人类学的创立者之一，拉德克利夫-布朗结构功能主义的追随者。他以研究南苏丹的阿赞德人和努尔人而闻名。

22. 保罗·福科内（1874—1938），法国社会学家，《社会学年鉴》的创刊成员之一。

23. 雷蒙德·弗斯（1901—2002），新西兰人类学家，在伦敦经济学院任教数十年，对《礼物》中莫斯对毛利人信仰的诠释提出质疑。

24. 詹姆斯·弗雷泽（1854—1941），苏格兰社会学家、人类学家，他认为人类思想发展遵循从巫术到宗教再到科学的演进顺序，并按照这一构想整理了一部 12 卷的世界各地宗教信仰全集《金枝》。《金枝》有 1890 年、1900 年和 1906—1915 年三个版本。

25. 欧内斯廷·弗里德尔（1920 年生），出生于匈牙利的美国人类学家，关注性别问题、希腊乡村和美国威斯康星州的齐佩瓦族。她因撰写了一篇极具开创性的名为《社会和性别角色》的文章而闻名。

26. 克利福德·格尔茨（1926—2006），美国人类学家，曾在印尼进行田野调查。他与维克多·特纳是公认的象征人类学和阐释人类学的创立者。

27. 莫里斯·古德利尔（1934 年生），法国哲学家、人类学家，曾在巴布亚新几内亚进行田野调查。他对经济人类学和发展人类学做出了贡献，在社会不公、性别和权力方面的研究分析也很出名。

28. 沃尔特·戈尔德施密特（1903—2010），美国人类学家，对田野调查兴趣浓厚，具有广泛的田野调查经验。他因分析农业产业与小型独立农场经济对加州当地社群的影响而闻名。

29. 奥克特·哈梅林（1856—1907），法国哲学家，任职于波尔多大学，是涂尔干的亲密盟友。

30. 罗伯特·赫兹（1881—1915），法国宗教社会学家，莫斯及涂尔干的

亲密同事，死于第一次世界大战。

31. 亨利·于贝尔（1872—1927），法国历史学家、社会学家，对宗教感兴趣，曾与莫斯密切合作，合写过多篇论文和书评。

32. 刘易斯·海德（1945 年生），美国作家、评论家和翻译家。他在创造力和商务方面的作品比较有名。

33. 理查德·海兰（1949 年生），美国作家、法学学者。在关于送礼的成文及不成文法律上的比较和历史分析方面比较有名。

34. 雅克·拉康（1901—1981），法国精神分析学家、社会学家、文学理论家和语言学家。他是后结构主义的中流砥柱。

35. 莫里斯·林哈德（1878—1954），法国牧师、人类学家，曾在法属新喀里多尼亚进行田野调查。他主张采用莫斯的方法论，被认为是美拉尼西亚人类学的创立者。

36. 克劳德·列维-斯特劳斯（1908—2009），法国社会学家，出生于比利时，也是"结构主义之父"。

37. 亨利·莱维-布律尔（1884—1964），法国社会学家，师从莫斯，他对法律比较、宗教和思维方式方面感兴趣。

38. 吕西安·莱维-布吕尔（1857—1939），法国哲学家、社会学家，对研究人类心灵进化历程感兴趣。他与莫斯、保罗·里韦一起在巴黎创立了民族学研究所。

39. 哈里·李伯森（1951 年生），美国历史学家，主要关注思想文化史、社会理论、旅行写作、宗教、创造力和礼物交换方面的内容。

40. 玛格丽特·洛克（1936 年生），英国出生的加拿大人类学家，专门研究医学人类学。她因其在老龄化、器官移植、比较医学方面的研究而闻名。

41. 布罗尼斯拉夫·马林诺夫斯基（1884—1942），波兰人类学家、社会学家和民族志学者，英国社会人类学的创立者之一（另一人是A. R. 拉德克利夫-布朗）。他因研究特罗布里恩群岛的"库拉圈"

而闻名。

42. 让-吕克·马利翁（1946 年生），法国哲学家，因其在宗教、爱情和礼物馈赠方面的研究而闻名。

43. 卡尔·马克思（1818—1883），极具影响力的经济学家和社会理论家，马克思主义理论源于他的作品，著名的《资本论》（1867—1894）和《共产党宣言》（1848），是一种强调阶级斗争的社会历史分析方法。

44. 玛格丽特·米德（1901—1978），美国人类学家，在美拉尼西亚和南太平洋地区开展关于性别角色、性行为、育儿和青春期的研究。

45. 约翰·斯图亚特·穆勒（1806—1873），英国公职人员、政治经济学家，认为个体在经济行为上的主动性和责任感是实现自由的基础。

46. 路易斯·亨利·摩尔根（1818—1881），美国律师、政治家、人类学家，按照社会进化论的思想（蒙昧期—野蛮期—文明期）研究亲缘关系、社会结构和习俗。

47. 丹尼丝·波尔姆（1909—1998），法国人，最早受过学术训练的女性人类学家之一。她是莫斯的学生，20 世纪 30 年代起，开始研究非洲的文学、礼仪以及社会政治的组织形式。

48. 卡尔·波兰尼（1886—1964），匈牙利裔美国哲学家、人类学家、社会历史学家和政治经济学家。他是"实质主义"的创立者，强调从特定的社会与文化角度出发研究经济活动，以 1944 年出版的《大转型》一书而为人所知。

49. A. R. 拉德克利夫-布朗（1881—1955），英国哲学家、心理学家、人类学家，被称为"英国结构功能主义之父"，与布罗尼斯拉夫·马林诺夫斯基一起创立了英国社会人类学。

50. 保罗·利科（1913—2005），法国哲学家，对历史、心理学、身份研究、语言、文学批评和神学研究感兴趣。他对基督教神学的研究受到了莫斯对互惠交换的分析的影响。

51. 保罗·里韦（1876—1958），法国医生、民族志学者，在南美进行研

究。他与莫斯、吕西安·列维-布吕尔一起在巴黎创立了民族学研究所。

52. 让·鲁什（1917—2004），法国人类学家、电影制作人，曾在非洲工作数十年，因其在电影拍摄中巧妙融入纪录片元素和虚构元素而闻名。

53. 马歇尔·萨林斯（1930 年生），美国人类学家，曾在太平洋地区进行田野调查，为人类学理论发展做出了突出贡献。他是芝加哥大学人类学和社会科学的名誉教授。

54. 费尔迪南·德·索绪尔（1857—1913），瑞士语言学家，现代语言学及意义生成研究的创立者，其著名的语言学演讲集在其去世后出版。

55. 艾伦·斯里福特（1955 年生），美国哲学家，对 19 世纪和 20 世纪的哲学研究及慷慨和馈赠主题颇感兴趣。

56. 莱斯利·夏普（1956 年生），美国医学人类学家，曾在马达加斯加做过田野调查。她因研究身体商品化和自我的社会建构而闻名。

57. 格奥尔格·西美尔（1858—1918），德国哲学家、社会学家，著有《货币哲学》，这是一本将经济系统视为社会和文化系统的开创性著作。

58. 赫伯特·斯宾塞（1820—1903），英国哲学家，进一步发展了进化论，认为物种、自然、社会和人的心灵都会从简单形态进化为复杂形态。

59. 玛丽莲·斯特拉森（1941 年生），英国人类学家，曾在巴布亚新几内亚进行田野调查。她在性别、亲缘关系、繁殖方面的研究工作对美拉尼西亚地区交换活动的早期人类学阐释提出了挑战。

60. 理查德·蒂特马斯（1907—1973），自学成才的英国学者，他在英国创立了社会政策学科，以研究社会和健康政策中的给予和利他主义精神而闻名。

61. 亚历克西·德·托克维尔（1805—1859），法国历史学家、政治理论家，他最著名的作品是《论美国的民主》（1835 年和 1840 年两版），是一本分析政治经济学和美国社会状况的作品。

62. **维克多·特纳**（1920—1983），苏格兰社会人类学家，以研究非洲的过渡仪式、礼制和象征物而闻名。他与克利福德·格尔茨是公认的象征人类学和阐释人类学的创立者。

63. **爱德华·伯内特·泰勒**（1832—1917），英国人类学家，将社会进化论思想拓展到文化研究领域，学术人类学的创立者之一。

64. **索尔斯坦·凡勃伦**（1857—1929），美国社会学家、经济学家，提出了"炫耀性消费"这一概念来描述竞争性的消费行为，著有《论有闲阶级》（1899 年）。

65. **马克斯·韦伯**（1864—1920），德国学者，在法律、哲学、经济学和社会学方面与莫斯志趣相投、研究相近，著有《新教伦理与资本主义精神》。

66. **安妮特·韦娜**（1933—1997），美国人类学家，于马林诺夫斯基特罗布里恩群岛田野调查 50 年后再次前往该岛进行调查，她以研究互惠式交换系统中女性所扮演的社会和政治角色而闻名。

67. **埃米尔·左拉**（1840—1902），法国小说家、剧作家，在小说中推崇自然主义。他因 1898 年的一封名为《我控诉》的信件而闻名，以捍卫被诬告的法国军官艾尔弗雷德·德雷福斯。

WAYS IN TO THE TEXT

- Marcel Mauss (1872–1950) was a French sociologist known for his contributions to the study of social behavior, his academic collaborations, and his political activism.

- *The Gift* showed that reciprocal* exchanges (the simultaneous exchange of gifts) are expressions of social relationships that bind individuals and groups through obligations that extend forward in time.

- The book is distinctive for the range of ethnographic* material described (that is, the depth of its study in terms of peoples and cultures), the significance of its findings, and the relevance of the analysis to social science, politics, and personal life.

Who Was Marcel Mauss?

Marcel Mauss, the author of *The Gift* (1923–4), was born in 1872 in Épinal, northeastern France. After leaving university he became an important figure in French academic sociology* (the study of social behavior) and remained so for 50 years. Mauss spent most of his life working on research projects, often in collaboration with other scholars, and editing professional journals. He was very active politically, too, joining the cooperative movement* (backing the idea that businesses should be owned by the people who work for them) and writing for socialist* publications; the general principles of socialism are that everyone has some share in the distribution of power and money. Mauss spoke out against anti-Semitism*—prejudice against Jewish people—and the abuse of political power. He spoke many languages and read ancient Greek, Latin, and Sanskrit.

After studying philosophy and law, Mauss worked closely with his uncle, Émile Durkheim,* an influential figure known as the "father of French sociology"; the two shared an interest in working out how people think by analyzing their cultural* beliefs, legal systems, and social institutions.*

On Durkheim's death in 1917, Mauss took over the journal that Durkheim had founded 20 years earlier, *L'Année Sociologique.** His book *The Gift*, discussing the relationship between his uncle's sociological theories, ancient laws, and recent data collected by anthropologists* (those who study humans, past and present, around the world), first appeared in the 1923–4 issue of this journal. The piece highlights the differences between one-off and ongoing exchanges between people, and offers a consideration of the relationship between economic activity, social behavior, belief systems, and notions of morality.

What Does *The Gift* Say?

Mauss's book *The Gift: The Form and Reason for Exchange in Archaic Societies* argues that people do not give things without expecting something back in return, either consciously or subconsciously. The analysis looks at the giving and receiving of objects, people, and intangible goods in archaic societies* (Mauss uses the term "archaic" to designate indigenous and ancient societies that operate without money but not without trade* and bartering*). Everyday economic transactions and larger cycles of gifts and return-gifts coexist in all societies; Mauss focuses on reciprocal transfers because they tie together individuals and groups in long-term relationships. His study focuses on societies in which everything from property to titles "is there for passing on, and for balancing accounts."[1]

Mauss highlights the intertwining of economic systems with social systems, politics, and morality. His analysis shows how precise laws and customs regulate exchanges in small, face-to-face societies and identifies similar patterns in earlier gift systems that have survived in industrialized societies. He concludes with the observation that looking at economic exchange from an anthropological point of view could influence public policy, and suggests that a fairer politico-economic system might come out of analyzing and expanding institutionalized forms of reciprocity—the principle of mutual exchange.

The Gift is an extremely detailed work in which Mauss analyzes each society's gift exchange rules within its own specific social, historical, and cultural context, reflecting his firmly held belief that all aspects of society deserve equal consideration—that is, that the study of material and technological factors is just as important as the study of religious and moral beliefs. *The Gift* shows how social systems and cultural beliefs help shape and give meaning to human behavior. These ideas also run through Mauss's other work on religion, seasonality* (changes in a society's activities according to season), and personhood* (the idea of being an individual).

One of the few texts that he wrote without a coauthor, *The Gift* is Mauss's most famous work. One of the ways his ideas spread was through a mutual exchange of ideas with work colleagues; in turn, those ideas spread through further exchanges with other people. But the case could be made that, had he been less of a collaborative scholar, he might have found more influence. Assessing Mauss's impact, two scholars of anthropological history note that he is "less well known than he might have been had his work appeared in a more compact form—it is scattered widely, most of it is short, and much of it is in collaboration, so that the value of his truly unusual contribution is hard to assess, although present-day social science is shot through with the results of his thinking."[2]

Mauss's short book has had an enormous impact on both academia and literature. The book has been translated into English three times, most recently in 2015. It continues to inspire intellectual activity throughout the humanities (fields such as languages, literature, and philosophy) and the social sciences (fields such as history, economics, and political science), and remains a pivotal text in sociology and anthropology.

Why Does *The Gift* Matter?

The Gift is useful for analyzing economic behavior in any setting. It provides insights into what motivates people and the meaning of economic concepts such as rationality* (in economics, a characteristic of reasoning in which costs and benefits are weighed so that the best decision might be made) and utility* (the usefulness of anything paid for). The book explores how economics and social and cultural systems affect each other. It is also relevant to studies of legal codes and political philosophy. The analysis provides a guide for understanding common themes across different sets of data. The last part of the book illustrates how events influence intellectual ideas. Mauss struggled to make sense of the political turmoil in Europe after World War I. His conclusions for Western society remain controversial and are relevant to the ethical concerns of the time.

The Gift provides food for thought on the meaning of gift-giving across cultures and the presumed lack of meaning of financial transactions beyond the purely functional. The book sheds light on the contradictory mixture of values that are part of giving, receiving, and giving in return. In reciprocal exchange, generosity and selflessness meet self-interest and binding obligation.

The book expands on gift-giving in our own society and any assumptions of purely unselfish motives, showing that it involves the values and expectations Mauss identifies in simpler societies. In personal life and in the workplace, transfers of favors and resources demand a return. They solidify relationships and bring both honor and status.

At the same time, the book shows that commercial transactions are not altogether disconnected from human relationships. Money itself is a cultural product supported by a specific social and legal framework. The book explains why money alone cannot compensate the giving that goes into paid labor—given the talent, creative energy, wisdom, knowledge, and so on that the laborer invests in his or her work. Likewise, financial measures alone do not capture many kinds of job performance. The book sheds light on what people's spending behavior achieves and says about them.

The Gift calls into question the assumption that individuals act and think in isolation.

The Gift is a book for all disciplines. It is a thorough analysis of a single topic that is also relevant to universal themes of existence. Whether in the lives of individuals or as the focus of intellectual analysis, reciprocal gift exchange is a human activity fraught with ambiguity. The book's staying power is a testament to our timeless fascination with social interaction.

---

1. Marcel Mauss, *The Gift: The Form and Reason for Exchange in Archaic Societies* (London: Routledge, 1990), 14.
2. Paul Bohanan and Mark Glazer (eds), *High Points in Anthropology* (New York: Alfred A. Knopf, 1988), 264.

SECTION 1
INFLUENCES

THE AUTHOR AND THE HISTORICAL CONTEXT

KEY POINTS

* Marcel Mauss's *The Gift* has had a lasting effect on the way anthropologists* and other scholars approach the analysis of cultures* in which economics, politics, technology, and individual motivations are intertwined.

* Mauss's academic training in sociology* (the study of social behavior, social institutions, and the origins and organization of human society), law, religion, and languages uniquely prepared him for comparative analyses* of cultural systems including gift exchange. In comparative analysis, research is conducted by a comparison of different systems, artifacts, or features.

* The political turmoil of the early twentieth century set the stage for Mauss's approach to ethnographic* material (information derived from the study of a group of people in the field—that is, in their own setting) and its implications for industrialized societies.

Why Read This Text?

Marcel Mauss's *The Gift: The Form and Reason for Exchange in Archaic Societies* concerns a topic close to everyone's heart: social relationships.[1] A second question is the degree to which individuals determine their own thoughts and actions as opposed to being controlled by society and culture. The book addresses both questions and contributes to scholarly knowledge about humans as members of groups.

Mauss explores the ways in which gifts and return gifts join people in cycles of exchange that are governed by rules and infused with cultural values. He provides a unifying interpretation of cross-cultural data and advances the sociological approach developed by his uncle, the pioneering sociologist Émile Durkheim.* Mauss's short book opens a window on the history of ideas, shares a wealth of fascinating ethnographic detail, and outlines a method for comparative analysis. The book provides food for thought on the connection between reciprocal* exchange (roughly, a system of mutual exchanges) and social cohesion—the stability enjoyed by a functioning society. Mauss reflects on what the study of small, face-to-face societies suggests about how to alter economic systems in industrialized societies for the common good.

In contrast to earlier scholars, Mauss showed that economic, political, religious, kinship* (the way in which a people formally recognizes relationships of different kinds), and other systems do not exist apart from one another. In line with Durkheim's thinking he focused on the shared ideas and institutionalized rules and procedures that form the context for individual beliefs and behaviors. Mauss did not foreground any single factor such as ecological forces or material constraints as the main force behind sociocultural systems. And although he accepted the idea that societies evolve and become more complicated, he made it very clear that complex societies were not necessarily better than simpler societies.

Mauss communicated his and Durkheim's ideas to colleagues and younger contemporaries such as the influential French anthropologist Claude Lévi-Strauss,* as well as students including the psychoanalyst and anthropologist Georges Devereux,* the pioneering anthropologist of Africa Denise Paulme,* and the filmmaker and anthropologist Jean Rouch.* Through them, Mauss's influence reached the thinkers Pierre Bourdieu,* Georges Condominas,* and many others.[2]

> "Where anthropology is concerned he [Mauss] would surely be more than satisfied. Nothing has been the same since. The big developments stem from this work."
> —— Mary Douglas,* "Foreword: No Free Gifts" in *The Gift*

Author's Life

Marcel Mauss was born in 1872 in Épinal, in the Lorraine region of northeastern France, to parents who both worked in textile businesses. Although his family was Orthodox Jewish, Mauss was not a religious man. His relatives included many scholars, most notably his maternal uncle, Émile Durkheim, who is considered the father of sociology. Mauss's much-younger cousin and Durkheim's niece, the marine biologist Claudette Raphael Bloch, was the mother of the British anthropologist Maurice Bloch* (born 1939).

After his university education in Bordeaux, where his uncle held France's first professorship in sociology and education, Mauss moved to Paris in 1895 to continue his studies. He spent two years (1897–8) traveling in England and the Netherlands before returning to Paris where he started lecturing in 1900, first at the École Pratique des Hautes Études, and after 1930 at the Collège de France.

Mauss actively engaged with the political upheavals that troubled Europe throughout his adult life. He joined the collectivist* student movement, the French Workers' Party,* and the Revolutionary Socialist Workers' Party,* all left-wing movements, and wrote for leftist publications including *La Vie Socialiste*, *Humanité*, and *Le Mouvement Socialiste*. Mauss wrote in support of the novelist and playwright Émile Zola,* whose public criticism of the French military for its anti-Semitism* (anti-Jewish sentiment) and military interference with legal procedure in the trial of Alfred Dreyfus* led to Dreyfus being cleared of the accusations made against him. Mauss continued to speak out against anti-Semitism and racism throughout his life, and his consciousness of political questions and dimensions are evident throughout his work, including in *The Gift*.[3]

Durkheim's death in 1917 was followed by a backlash against the curricular changes he had helped institute throughout France as a professor of pedagogy (the method and practice of teaching). Mauss, an advocate of Durkheim's sociological approach, retreated into administrative activity. He took over direction of the journal *L'Année Sociologique*,* which had been founded by Durkheim in 1898 and had lost many of its main contributors to World War I* (1914–18), including the sociologists Henri Beauchat* and Robert Hertz.* In 1925–6, Mauss cofounded the Institut d'Ethnologie* at the University of Paris with the ethnographer Paul Rivet* and the sociologist Lucien Lévy-Bruhl.* Mauss co-directed and lectured at the Institut until 1939. World War II* (1939–45) brought Mauss further losses and grief, which, combined with personal and domestic troubles, led him to cease his scholarly work. He died in Paris in 1950.[4]

Author's Background

Marcel Mauss was a broadly trained scholar who learned many languages including Russian, Greek, Sanskrit, Latin, and Malayo-Polynesian. At the University of Bordeaux he studied philosophy and law. After coming in third place in the civil service examination in 1895, Mauss chose to pursue further education at the École Pratique des Hautes Études in Paris, one of France's publicly funded selective academic and research institutes. Mauss studied comparative religion and ancient Greek, Roman, Indian, and Germanic literature and philosophy. Between 1897 and 1898 he traveled to the Netherlands and England, where he worked briefly with Edward Burnett Tylor,* the first university professor of anthropology in Britain. Tylor's holistic* definition of culture— a definition of culture concerned with the interdependence of its components—continues to be cited today, though with important caveats about variability and change.[5]

From 1902 to 1930, Mauss taught a course on "L'histoire des religions des peuples non-civilisés" ("The History of the Religions of Non-Civilized Peoples") at the École Pratique des Hautes Études. From 1930 to 1939 he offered the same course at the Collège de France, another of France's prestigious seats of learning.[6] His enduring interest in comparative religion contributed to his work on gift exchange as a social phenomenon.

During the early interwar years, Mauss continued to explore

political philosophy as a socialist* and member of the cooperative movement* in France (a movement in which workers coowned the companies they worked for). In *The Gift*, Mauss defends individualism as a motivator of productive activity and social participation, but points out the exploitation that is possible where transactions are construed as separate from their moral and social context.

1. Marcel Mauss, *The Gift: The Form and Reason for Exchange in Archaic Societies* (London: Routledge, 1990).

2. Mary Douglas, "Foreword: No Free Gifts," in *The Gift* by Marcel Mauss (London: Routledge, 2000); Walter Goldschmidt, "Untitled Review of *The Gift* by Marcel Mauss," *American Anthropologist* 57, no. 6 (1955): 1299–1300; Seth Leacock, "The Ethnological Theory of Marcel Mauss," *American Anthropologist* 56 (1954): 58–71.

3. Marcel Fournier, *Marcel Mauss: A Biography* (Princeton, NJ: Princeton University Press, 2005), 4.

4. Paul Bohannan and Mark Glazer (eds), *High Points in Anthropology* (New York: Alfred A. Knopf, 1988), 264–6; Goldschmidt, "Untitled Review," 1299; Leacock, "The Ethnological Theory," 58–9, 64–5.

5. "Culture or Civilization, taken in its wide ethnographic sense, is that complex whole which includes knowledge, belief, art, morals, law, custom, and any other capabilities and habits acquired by man as a member of society." Edward Burnett Tylor, *Primitive Culture: Researches into the Development of Mythology, Philosophy, Religion, Art, and Custom* (London: J. Murray, 1871), 1.

6. Upon succeeding Mauss at the École Pratique des Hautes Études, Lévi-Strauss renamed the course "Comparative Religion of Non-Literate Peoples."

ACADEMIC CONTEXT

KEY POINTS

• Anthropology* is the study of the biological and cultural history and current variability of humankind. *The Gift* is a comparative study of gift exchange as a central institution*—in the sense of a conventionalized activity—that structures relationships and channels the flow of goods, people, and intangibles such as rituals and titles.

• In the early twentieth century, sociologists* (scholars of the history and structure of society) and anthropologists sought both to document the features of non-Western societies and to classify and make sense of the information in terms of social evolutionary* stages (according to social evolutionary principles, societies progress through a fixed series of stages of ever-increasing technological, social, and intellectual perfection).

• Marcel Mauss collaborated with scholars including the sociologists Paul Fauconnet* and Émile Durkheim* seeking to identify overarching patterns to cultural institutions.

The Work in its Context

At the time of Marcel Mauss's writing of *The Gift*, French sociology was dominated by the work of Mauss's uncle, Émile Durkheim. The backdrop for Durkheim's sociology, in turn, was French philosophy's turn-of-the-century rejection of English utilitarianism*—a philosophical and liberal* political tradition that presumed individual rationality* was the elemental, positive force driving modern economic life.[1] French philosophers argued that radical individualism failed to account for the social context of individual actions and beliefs. That is, the British view ignored the relationship between economic and social organization, and overlooked how cultural beliefs and social position could affect the choices an individual makes. French philosophers including Alexis de Tocqueville* argued that radical individualism led to exploitation and resulted in people being alienated from society and disengaged from politics.

Durkheim proposed a middle ground between thinking of an individual as separate from society and seeing him or her as being completely controlled by social context. Although critics have often concluded that the individual was unimportant to his sociological science, Durkheim was intensely interested in the degree to which the political and social systems of different types of society allowed individual personhood* to flourish. Durkheim focused on identifying shared norms and rules and assessing their effect on individual choice. He did not dismiss the force of individual will, but as a sociologist his task was to explain social dynamics and identify collective representations* (shared beliefs and understandings). Together with Paul Fauconnet, Mauss laid out Durkheim's theoretical approach in a 1901 article for the French encyclopedia *La Grande Encyclopédie*.[2]

Although he worked with material from small, non-Western societies, Mauss considered himself a sociologist. French sociology continued to encompass anthropology long after the latter became a separate science elsewhere.[3] In the United Kingdom and United

States, anthropology was concerned with the comparative study of all societies and especially non-Western ones, whereas sociology tended to focus on the internal workings of industrialized societies.

> "In the economic and legal systems that have preceded our own, one hardly ever finds a simple exchange of goods, wealth, and products in transactions concluded by individuals. First, it is not individuals but collectivities that impose obligations of exchange and contract upon each other ... Moreover, what they exchange is not solely property and wealth, movable and immovable goods, and things economically useful. In particular, such exchanges are acts of politeness ... Finally, these total services and counter-services are committed to in a somewhat voluntary form by presents and gifts, although in the final analysis they are strictly compulsory, on pain of private or public warfare."
>
> —— Marcel Mauss, *The Gift: The Form and Reason for Exchange in Archaic Societies*

Overview of the Field

Durkheim's 1897 book *On Suicide*, for which Mauss compiled the data, illustrated the effect of social forces on individual behavior.[4] Durkheim's analysis of the variability in suicide rates across social groups, nations, and time showed that mental distress did just not occur randomly as a result of biological or chance factors. The study illustrated his trademark analytical approach, shared by Mauss: empirical,* objective, detailed examination of working systems in all their complexity ("empirical" study is research founded on evidence verifiable by observation). Durkheim and Mauss were ahead of their time in recognizing that their own inherited collective representations and politico-economic systems affected their interpretation of other cultures.*

Their caution is evident in Mauss's uncertainty about social evolution. He taught that all societies were civilized, albeit in different ways.[5] This was a clear departure from the progressive logic of nineteenth- and early twentieth-century explorers, missionaries, and theorists such as the British philosopher Herbert Spencer* and the US anthropologist Lewis Henry Morgan,* who believed societies could be ranked like animal species into forms of ever-increasing complexity and perfection.[6] To illustrate, while remarking on the similarities in gift exchange across societies widely dispersed around the Pacific Ocean, Mauss notes the presence of comparable systems in Africa, Asia, and the Americas. In *The Gift*, he refuses to engage in the ongoing debate about whether similar customs in different societies are the result of diffusion or independent invention.[7]

Mauss does, however, concentrate his study on existing archaic societies* similarly placed on an evolutionary scale. He also looks at societies that came before modern Indo-European societies and searches for "survivals" in present-day customs (that is, features that have endured from ancient social practices). Looking backward, he proposes a model for how the primordial societies managed economic exchanges. Yet throughout the three-stage progression Mauss finds that the same basic principles apply, and therefore that no society is superior to another.

Academic Influences

At the time of Mauss's writing, anthropology had moved from the study to the field. *The Gift* was made possible by the on-the-ground work of anthropologists such as Bronislaw Malinowski* in the Pacific Trobriand Islands and Franz Boas* along the Northwest Coast of North America. Mauss's approach to the material was the product of many influences. At Bordeaux, these included the philosophers Alfred Victor Espinas,* who studied the collective genius behind technological and cultural traditions and forms, and the philosopher Octave Hamelin,* who was interested in the binding effect of human relationships.[8] Mauss collaborated on research with Durkheim and other members of the original group of contributors to the influential journal *L'Année Sociologique.**

While Mauss shared the prevailing view that it was useful to examine simpler or more "primitive" forms of social facts because they show the basic features of the later ones, he did not agree with people—including Morgan—who said civilizations always progressed onward and upward, from barbarism to savagery to civilization.[9] Likewise, Mauss's course on comparative religion at the École Pratique des Hautes Études departed from the standard teachings encapsulated by the Scottish anthropologist James Frazer's* 12-volume *The Golden Bough*.[10] Frazer believed that human thought progressed from primitive magic to religion and finally to science, abandoning the logic of affinity* (the principle of "like attracts like") and contagion* (the principle in "primitive" magic that mystical forces are present in things such as body products, and can be manipulated for magical purposes) for true understanding of cause and effect. Mauss rejected Frazer's framework along with his method of ethnological* comparison (the comparison of material produced by the systematic study of a particular people) in which he used snippets of material out of context and combined them to suit his aims.[11]

Mauss's approach was methodical and evidence-based. Like Boas, he resisted deductive (or top-down) theories about the impact of evolutionary, psychological, geographical, racial, or economic forces on social systems and individual behavior.[12] Mauss preferred Durkheim's method of searching within and across cases for social systems, politico-legal institutions, and shared beliefs that set the parameters for action without simply dictating it.

1. Mary Douglas, "Foreword: No Free Gifts," in *The Gift* by Marcel Mauss (London: Routledge, 2000).

2. Paul Fauconnet and Marcel Mauss, "Sociologie: Objet et Méthode," *La Grande Encyclopédie* 30 (1901): 165–76.

3. Seth Leacock, "The Ethnological Theory of Marcel Mauss," *American Anthropologist* 56 (1954): 60.

4. Émile Durkheim, *On Suicide* (London: Penguin Books, 2006).

5. Leacock, "The Ethnological Theory," 60.

6. Lewis Henry Morgan, *Ancient Society: Researches into the Lines of Human Progress from Savagery through Barbarism to Civilization* (New York: Henry Holt, 1877).

7. Marcel Mauss, *The Gift: The Form and Reason for Exchange in Archaic Societies* (London: Routledge, 1990), 97–8.

8. Paul Bohannan and Mark Glazer (eds), *High Points in Anthropology* (New York: Alfred A. Knopf, 1988), 264.

9. For instance, Morgan was so certain of the progression of societies from savagery to barbarism to civilization that he invented taxonomic categories without evidence. He assumed that sooner or later the requisite social customs or kinship systems would be found to fill in the gaps. Morgan, *Ancient Society*.

10. James George Frazer, *The Golden Bough* (New York: Simon and Schuster, 1996).

11. Marcel Mauss, "L'Enseignement de l'Histoire des Religions des Peuples Non-Civilisés à l'École des Hautes Études," *Revue de l'Histoire des Religions* 45 (1902): 36–55; Fredrik Barth et al., *One Discipline, Four Ways: British, German, French, and American Anthropology* (Chicago: University of Chicago Press, 2005); Leacock, "The Ethnological Theory," 61.

12. Franz Boas, *Race, Language, and Culture* (London: Collier-Macmillan, 1940).

MODULE 3
THE PROBLEM

KEY POINTS

• The overarching question that sociologists* sought to address at the time of Mauss's analysis of *The Gift* was how societies are organized and how their structure is related to the way they function.

• Some scholars assumed that societies evolved through a fixed series of technological, social, and intellectual advances; for others, social forms were determined by material, technological, or biological factors; others still concentrated on documenting languages, customs, and ways of life in all their historical and local particularity.

• Mauss focused on the exchange of property, persons, and services in societies believed to occupy the same social evolutionary level. He sought regularities across cases but considered each one in context, without speculating on ultimate causes.

Core Question

The core question that Marcel Mauss addresses in *The Gift* is: what is the purpose, meaning, and legal ordering of exchange in societies without money or laws governing contracts? Mauss found that ethnographers*—those engaged in the study of people and their culture—were often perplexed that people in archaic societies* (indigenous and similar, extinct, societies), followed precise rules about how gifts were to be offered, accepted, and repaid. What seemed to escape the outsiders' notice was that exchange involved time scales and interconnected moral and material transfers that, once mapped out, revealed the contours, hierarchies, dynamism, and cohesion of a given society.

The topic of exchange was related to a question about individuality that interested Émile Durkheim.* Both Durkheim and Mauss believed that individual personhood* was relatively undeveloped in the simplest societies, in which the family or clan* (relatives sharing a common ancestor) was everything and solidarity*—connectedness—was "mechanical," or the automatic result of low specialization of tasks and roles. At the opposite extreme, in industrialized societies individual personhood was elevated to excess; social relations enveloped people but were not acknowledged. Here "organic" solidarity came about through the interdependence of specialized functions. Individuality, rather than belonging, was everything.[1]

While Durkheim assumed that individual personhood in societies between these extremes remained trapped beneath a dense net of social ties and cultural beliefs, Mauss showed that individuals are motivated to participate in gift exchange by a mixture of prestige and honor with material gain. They exercise self-interest. Moreover, interactions as a whole represent a system that is consistent and predictable, even in contexts without market* transactions (that is, in contexts where things are exchanged purely according to agreed values). In either case, exchange is connected to status, but while reciprocal* giving is public and observable and therefore more exacting about fairness, market exchange is hidden and consequently further removed from personal and group honor.

Mauss concludes that, fundamentally, we are all the same—it is just social context that makes us behave differently. So the differences are ones of degree, not kind, and he suggests that market societies should revive the mutually binding elements of economic exchange in the interests of individual and collective well-being.[2]

> *"The subject is clear. In Scandinavian civilization, and in a good number of others, exchanges and contracts take place in the form of presents; in theory these are voluntary, in reality they are given and reciprocated obligatorily."*
> —— Marcel Mauss, *The Gift: The Form and Reason for Exchange in Archaic Societies*

The Participants

Mauss spent his entire career collaborating closely with other scholars. His work reveals a trajectory of thought that is both shared and distinctive. The results are evident in *The Gift*.

Mauss's 1903 article coauthored with Durkheim, *Primitive Classification*, explores how simple societies categorize objects, people, and phenomena.[3] The authors propose a connection between logical categories and social divisions such as those between men and women or between clans and tribes* (a category in a society politically organized around kinship* relations and classes). In other words, conceptual and linguistic categories are not inherent in the nature of things but are, rather, socially constructed.

Mauss and Durkheim extended these ideas to a developing

theory of the sacred*—the sphere of ideas, rituals, and objects considered worthy of religious veneration. Durkheim's 1912 book on comparative religion, *The Elementary Forms of the Religious Life*, explores how society symbolizes itself in "totems"*— inert objects conceptually transformed into sacred things with mystical power—with the result that social categories are mapped onto nature.[4] Mauss and the historian and sociologist Henri Hubert's* 1899 work on animal sacrifice in ancient India and early Judaism,"Essai sur la Nature et la Fonction du Sacrifice" ("Essay on the Nature and Function of Sacrifice"), identifies the concept of the *sacré* (sacred), which grants the sacrificial gift the power to demand a return gift from the gods.[5] Their 1904 publication on magic, *A General Theory of Magic*, focuses on the Polynesian* and Australo-Melanesian* concept of *mana*: *[6] the mobile spiritual force that pervades the universe, attaches to objects, and reveals itself through some people's advantages and powers.[7]

In a 1906 article on Eskimo* (Inuit) migrations written with the sociologist Henri Beauchat,* *Seasonal Variation of the Eskimo: A Study in Social Morphology*, Mauss shows that the customs governing winter convergence and summer dispersal of groups cannot be explained in simple ecological terms such as the availability of animals to hunt.[8] Mauss and Beauchat argue that the same principle applies to the seasonal variability in activity among other populations. The article contributes to a body of work that established the social origins of beliefs and practices that other scholars saw as the result of biological needs, universal mental constructs, or the physical laws of nature.

The Contemporary Debate

Mauss's analysis in *The Gift* is based on the work of scholars including Bronislaw Malinowski* in the Pacific Trobriand Islands, the British philosopher and anthropologist* A. R. Radcliffe-Brown* in the Andaman Islands and Western Australia, and the German American anthropologist Franz Boas* on the Northwest Coast of North America.[9] Each of these ethnographers had a profound impact on anthropology and sociology.

Radcliffe-Brown drew upon Durkheim's thoughts about collective representations and social institutions* in his development of British structural-functionalism.*[10] Structural-functionalism is based on an analogy between society and the human body. The will or actions of individual people—compared to cells in the analogy—do not fundamentally alter the system, at least not on their own. Malinowski, who with Radcliffe-Brown founded British social anthropology (the comparative analysis* of human societies), differed from this school of thought in giving more weight to the individual and in his belief that society is born out of basic human biological and psychological needs.[11]

Franz Boas took a different approach to ethnography known as historical particularism.* Boas avoided deductive theorizing in favor of thorough data collection and intensive study of indigenous* languages (the languages spoken by a place's first inhabitants).[12] Through the use of evidence verifiable by observation, Boas demonstrated change through examples such as kinship* systems (systems that define how people are related), art forms, and even

119

head shape, and in the process challenged prevailing racial and evolutionary theories and the idea that societies tend to remain stable through automatic regulation of internal variables.[13]

Mauss's analysis of gift exchange combines elements from each of these perspectives. Mauss takes structural-functionalist premises for granted but also accounts for individual motivation. In line with Boas, he resists the idea that some societies or customs are superior to others and examines institutions in context, pays attention to change, and does not take a deterministic view of causation (that is, the idea that one or more variables directly produces a specific outcome). At the same time Mauss focuses on similarities between cultures in order to support general laws and sustain a loosely evolutionary progression from simpler to more complex societies.

1. Émile Durkheim, *The Division of Labor in Society* (New York: Free Press, 1984).

2. Marcel Mauss, *The Gift: The Form and Reason for Exchange in Archaic Societies* (London: Routledge, 1990).

3. Émile Durkheim and Marcel Mauss, *Primitive Classification* (Chicago: University of Chicago Press, 1963).

4. Émile Durkheim, *The Elementary Forms of the Religious Life* (New York: Free Press, 1915).

5. Marcel Mauss and Henri Hubert, "Essai sur la Nature et la Fonction du Sacrifice," *L'Année Sociologique* (1897–98): 29–138.

6. Marcel Mauss and Henri Hubert, *A General Theory of Magic* (London: Routledge, 2001).

7. Durkheim, *The Elementary Forms*, 223.

8. Marcel Mauss and Henri Beauchat, *Seasonal Variation of the Eskimo: A Study in Social Morphology* (London: Routledge, 1979).

9. Malinowski's treatise on inter-island exchange relationships in the Trobriand Islands appeared three

years before *The Gift*. In the same year, Radcliffe-Brown published the final analysis of fieldwork completed some 15 years before in the Andaman Islands; a decade earlier, he had published the results of fieldwork in Western Australia. Boas published articles and books on the populations of the Northwest Coast of North America from the late nineteenth century through 1940.

10. Alfred Reginald Radcliffe-Brown, *The Andaman Islanders* (Cambridge: Cambridge University Press, 1933).

11. Bronislaw Malinowski, *Argonauts of the Western Pacific: An Account of Native Enterprise and Adventure in the Archipelagos of Melanesian New Guinea* (London: Routledge, 1922).

12. Franz Boas, "The Limitations of the Comparative Method of Anthropology," *Science* 4, no. 103 (1896): 901–8; Franz Boas, "Changes in Bodily Form of Descendants of Immigrants," *American Anthropologist* 14, no. 3 (1912): 530–62.

13. See for example Boas's discussion of patrilineal and matrilineal kinship among tribes of the Northwest Coast of North America: Franz Boas, *Kwakiutl Ethnography* (Chicago: University of Chicago Press, 1966).

THE AUTHOR'S CONTRIBUTION

KEY POINTS

* Mauss shows that societies without modern forms of currency* (a medium of exchange such as cash, or shells, say) nonetheless have legal, political, and economic systems that regulate the flow of goods and services.

* By explaining the moral and material aspects of exchange in face-to-face societies, Mauss identifies a common thread in diverse ethnographic* studies and provides a model for understanding human interaction in mass society.

* The analysis unites state-of-the-art theoretical perspectives on social institutions* (codified relationships or activities) and collective representations* (shared beliefs and understandings) with contemporary methods of empirical* research and comparative analysis.* Comparative analysis requires the examination of two or more cases to identify similarities and differences that might explain their respective outcomes.

Author's Aims

Marcel Mauss's aim in *The Gift* is to explain the binding obligations created by gift exchange in simple societies. To this end, he combines ethnographic evidence gathered by other scholars with his own studies of ancient languages and philosophies. His analysis focuses on the shared features among norms governing exchange relationships across societies.

Mauss shows that simple societies have devised rules that structure the transfer of valuables of all kinds, tangible and intangible. The institution of gift exchange is related to other social institutions such as marriage or religious practices and contributes to social solidarity* (support and connectedness) and stability. By identifying the legal, social, political, and moral aspects of economic exchange, Mauss sheds a new light on the concepts of utility* (in economics, the material or psychological usefulness of purchased goods to the purchaser) and rational* self-interest (the weighing of costs and benefits to arrive at a decision). Participation in gift cycles is at once voluntary and obligatory, rewarding and costly, material and spiritual. Mauss also shows that the economic exchange systems of simple and complex societies are not radically different but rather operate according to similar principles. Complex societies contain remnants of the more socially significant economic exchanges characteristic of simpler societies.

The structure of the book clearly reflects the author's aims and approach. Mauss begins by describing a basic system of generalized give-and-take or reciprocity* (the principle that acts or material gifts should be met with a return, often in a formalized or cyclical fashion) in small societies throughout the world. He then analyzes an extremely competitive form characterized by built-in escalation—that each gift be greater than the last, not just equivalent—and even the destruction of property as a display of status. Mauss demonstrates the survival of similar practices in the languages, laws, and customs of modern descendants of ancient civilizations. Finally, he assesses the failures of modern politico-economic systems and considers what simpler societies can teach complex ones about protecting social welfare and improving interpersonal relationships.

Mauss achieves his principal objectives in *The Gift*. The main arguments are backed up by a good deal of empirical evidence (evidence verifiable by observation). However, the conclusions are more speculative due to the lack of comparable data on industrialized societies.

> "The circulation of goods follows that of men, women, and children, of feasts, rituals, ceremonies, and dances, and even that of jokes and insults. All in all, it is one and the same. If one gives things and returns them, it is because one is giving and receiving 'respects'—we still say 'courtesies.' Yet, it is also because by giving one is giving oneself, and if one gives oneself, it is because one 'owes' oneself—one's person and one's goods—to others."
>
> —— Marcel Mauss, *The Gift: The Form and Reason for Exchange in Archaic Societies*

Approach

To analyze the middle level of social evolution*—according to which societies advance in recognizable states to increased sophistication—Mauss hypothesizes an earlier phase in which individuality was completely subordinated to the family or clan.* Groups were bound to each other by systems of *"préstations totales"* or "total services." These included all things exchanged between them: goods, courtesies, marriage partners, meals, and intangibles such as dances, titles, names, and rituals.

Mauss explains that the gift exchange systems of existing and historical archaic societies* developed out of the total services system but involve larger territories and higher-order political units such as tribes.* Trade* (the formalized exchange of unalike items according to prescribed standards of value) and barter* (the exchange of dissimilar items on the spot and possibly involving bargaining) occur alongside gift exchange, reflecting the emergence of individual personhood.* In complex agricultural and industrial societies, individuality develops further as family and social bonds weaken due to modern forms of anonymous transactions mediated by abstract currency.[1]

Mauss illustrates the system of total services through examples such as thanksgiving feasts and gift sacrifice in Polynesia,* Australia and New Zealand, Malaysia, the far north of Eurasia, Africa, and the Americas. He then describes a class of competitive gift cycles he names after the *potlatch** system of feasts along the Northwest Coast of North America, a means to display wealth in which increasingly expensive gifts were handed over, and objects sometimes destroyed.

Mauss explains that comparable systems are common in Papua New Guinea and elsewhere in Melanesia.* In addition, many seemingly elementary systems of total services are really intermediate forms marked by escalation.[2] Such mild *potlatch* systems exist in Australia, Fiji, southern Asia, and among what he calls the Pygmies.* Traces remain in the laws and customs of ancient Rome, India, Germanic populations, and China.[3]

Lastly, Mauss analyzes "survivals" (enduring traces of ancient ideas or practices) in languages and laws derived from ancient Semitic, Greek, Roman, Indian, Germanic, Celtic, and Chinese civilizations. He shows that reciprocity and social institutions continue to sustain old systems of obligation and entitlement through gifts. However, in complex society individuality prevails due to the predominance of exchange formalized through money and contract law.

Contribution in Context

Mauss's analysis generated original insights about gift exchange and social relationships across ethnographic settings. To illustrate, Mauss provides a unified explanation for the competitive escalating systems of feasts and gifts that he describes as *"préstations totales agonistique."* These include the *kula** ring, by which wealth objects move among the Trobriand Islands, and the *potlatch* system of feasts on the Northwest Coast of North America.

The kula described by Bronislaw Malinowski* involves the circulation of decorated white shell armbands and red shell disc necklaces carried by canoe in opposite directions from one Trobriand island to another.[4] There is bartering for everyday goods but only the gift objects carry invisible spiritual qualities, confer prestige rather than use value, and are paid back after a time lag. The value of the armbands and necklaces rises by having been previously held by esteemed people such as respected "big men," and is independent of their aesthetic qualities.

Likewise, the gifts exchanged through the Northwest Coast potlatch system of feasts described by Franz Boas* carry spiritual force. Copper is especially valued because it attracts other copper objects. The potlatch is unique for its extremes of competitiveness. To really "flatten" a rival chief and tribe, the hosts may destroy huge amounts of their own valuable property: blankets, food, houses, and copper objects thrown into the sea. Here Mauss shows how gifts that cannot be returned increase the prestige of the giver and humiliate the receiver.[5]

Mauss shows how these different gift cycles express the same patterns of moral and material transfer. He identifies the distinction already present in simpler societies between one-off commodity transactions and gifts in which the individual and larger society are involved.[6] Mauss's comparative analysis reveals that the flow of transfers is orderly and meaningful in all societies.

---

1. Marcel Mauss, *The Gift: The Form and Reason for Exchange in Archaic Societies* (London: Routledge, 1990), 5–6, 46, 82–3.
2. Mauss, *The Gift*, 7.
3. Mauss, *The Gift*, 7, 19, 97–8.
4. Bronislaw Malinowski, *Argonauts of the Western Pacific: An Account of Native Enterprise and Adventure in the Archipelagos of Melanesian New Guinea* (London: Routledge, 1922).
5. Mauss, *The Gift*, 37, 74, 86–8.
6. Mauss, *The Gift*, 11.

SECTION 2
IDEAS

MAIN IDEAS

KEY POINTS

* Mauss shows that gifts are not simply presents given out of generosity but tools for building social relationships. The obligations carried by gift exchange connect people in positive and negative ways.

* Gift exchange is what makes face-to-face societies tick: it fuels and structures economic, social, religious, and political life. Gift cycles either create mutual obligations or, if interrupted, result in gains in honor and status for the donor at the expense of the receiver.

* Mauss demonstrates how reciprocal exchanges bind individuals and groups but also protect their autonomy, whereas commercial transactions are more favorable to exploitation. The balance between the two influences the level of social cohesiveness and the quality of human interactions.

Key Themes

The focus of Marcel Mauss's analysis in *The Gift* is small-scale or archaic societies* throughout the world but especially in the Pacific region of Melanesia,* Northwest North America, and ancient Eurasia.* Mauss shows how the obligation to give, to receive, and, after a set period of time, to return gifts sustains long-term social relationships that bind individuals and groups in positive and negative ways. The force that compels exchange derives from unwritten but nonetheless formal legal principles, cultural beliefs about honor and prestige, and the symbolic meanings conveyed by the objects and nonmaterial goods that pass between parties. The blending of material, human, and magical or spiritual elements makes economic activity inseparable from social, religious, and political systems and relationships.

The fundamental principle behind the entire system of gift exchange is the concept that "one good turn deserves another," or reciprocity.* It is the same idea behind the expression,"there's no such thing as a free lunch."These "survivals" of an earlier historical period in European and American culture seem to show that regardless of what sort of society people live in, gift-giving is a complicated process, with the gift itself full of all sorts of mixed messages and not necessarily a physical object. For example, even the very words "gift" and "present" might signify donations such as time and knowledge or talents such as musical ability.

Mauss focuses on how reciprocity contributes to social cohesion in small, face-to-face societies in which—unlike in market* societies where labor, land, goods, and services are calculated in units of currency—exchanges are characterized by personal and social meaning and obligation; these exchanges are, further, motivated by things such as prestige, duty, honor, sacrifice, generosity, and self-interest. The things that change hands include tangible goods (physical things such as jewelry, housewares, and clothing); food and drink, often shared between parties; and intangible things such as hospitality, dances, names, titles, and rituals. Gifts must be returned with equivalent or better gifts, which may be something completely different to the original gift. In all cases gifts are calculated according to established systems of value, which include qualities that may or may not embrace utilitarian considerations. The sum total of these laws and rules is nothing less than a map of the society and its connections to others.[1]

> "What rule of legality and self-interest, in societies of a backward or archaic type, compels the gift that has been received to be obligatorily reciprocated? What power resides in the object given that causes its recipient to pay it back?"
> —— Marcel Mauss, *The Gift: The Form and Reason for Exchange in Archaic Societies*

Exploring the Ideas

Basing his analysis on gift exchange, Mauss shows that culture plays a major role in shaping human behavior. In contrast to the then-current notion that social features were determined by ecological, material, and biological factors, Mauss focuses on social institutions* and cultural beliefs or collective representations* (shared beliefs and understandings) as he did in earlier work on magic and religion. Through the "total social phenomenon" or "total social fact" of gift exchange, Mauss illustrates Émile Durkheim's* belief that the institutions of simple societies serve to maintain social stability and solidarity.*Therefore, social cohesiveness (the closeness of relationships among members of a society) requires that individuals accept being constrained in their behavior by systematic and long-term obligations to others. Reciprocal exchange, however, still allows individuals to exercise self-interest.

Gift cycles hold small, face-to-face societies together, even while revealing and reinforcing hierarchies and inequalities between and within them. Continuous reciprocal exchange is the opposite of discrete sales mediated by money and moneyless transactions through barter* (the exchange of dissimilar items) or trade* (the formalized exchange of dissimilar items according to prescribed standards of value). In other words, the contrast is between reciprocal exchange, which involves open-ended time scales and items whose values are not reckoned in terms of currency, and one-time exchanges where values are balanced either because, for instance, a certain number of bananas is worth a certain number of shells, or there is currency to do the work of translating commodity values into units. Mauss also shows that trade is not unknown to simple societies and that credit is built into the gift cycle through ratcheting values and delayed repayment, which is like interest. In sum, economic activity, including gift exchange, is structured according to similar principles across all kinds of societies.

Mauss suggests that comparing and contrasting gift exchange across various societies highlights principles that can guide us all and lead to a better society, and that indicate that not all progress is positive.[2] In advanced civilizations, where economics is seen as a straightforward matter of cash and contract, people fail to recognize and cultivate reciprocity. People in Western societies, he says, are more isolated, whereas people in simpler societies are more interconnected but nonetheless maintain their autonomy. The point is that the Western system does not promote reciprocal material and spiritual exchange to the degree it could. As a result, people are more distanced from one another, and there is lower social solidarity. Mauss applauds the simpler groups and populations who "have learnt how to oppose and to give to one another without sacrificing themselves to one another," concluding that this is "what tomorrow, in our so-called civilized world, classes and nations and individuals also, must learn. This is one of the enduring secrets of their wisdom and solidarity."[3]

Language and Expression

The Gift is a deceptively short essay of around one hundred pages of text complemented by a roughly equal quantity of notes. The essay first appeared in 1923–4 in *L'Année Sociologique.** Publication of the journal had been suspended since World War I* due to the deaths of several main contributors including the journal's founder, Durkheim. Mauss had collaborated with this group on a variety of projects and was determined to carry their collective scholarly legacy forward. His contribution to the revived journal speaks to an audience that would have included them, had they been alive.

The original title of *The Gift* was *Essai sur le don: forme et raison de l'échange dans les sociétés archaïques—Essay on the Gift: The Form and Reason of Exchange in Archaic Societies.* Mauss's choice of the word "essay" reflects his intention to present an argument in a concise and orderly, but not overly academic, way. But the work is written for people who already have a basic knowledge of early twentieth-century sociology and anthropology.* For today's readers, previous knowledge of contemporary sociological theory and the ethnographic* material discussed in the book is helpful but not necessary. The notes help fill in the picture. The 1954 English translation is very much written in the formal language of the day, whereas the 1990 translation cited in this analysis is a less close fit to the spirit and content of the original.[4]

---

1. Mary Douglas, "Foreword: No Free Gifts," in *The Gift* by Marcel Mauss (London: Routledge, 2000), viii.

2. Marcel Mauss, *The Gift: The Form and Reason for Exchange in Archaic Societies* (London: Routledge, 1990), 77.

3. Mauss, *The Gift*, 82–3.

4. For an illustration, see the two translations of Mauss's sentence beginning with "Les clans, les âges et, généralement, les sexes." Marcel Mauss, "Essai sur le Don: Forme et Raison de l'Échange dans les Sociétés Archaïques," *L'Année Sociologique* no. 1 (1923–4): 97; Marcel Mauss, *The Gift: Forms and Functions of Exchange in Archaic Societies* (Glencoe, IL: Free Press (1954), 70; Marcel Mauss, *The Gift: The Form and Reason for Exchange in Archaic Societies* (London: Routledge, 1990), 72.

SECONDARY IDEAS

KEY POINTS

* In addition to the political and legal structures that sustain social relationships built through gift exchange, Mauss identifies a transcendent quality of gifts (a quality that cannot be quantified in exclusively physical terms) that motivates people to keep them in circulation.

* Cultural beliefs about the mystical properties of gifts favor compliance and therefore social solidarity* and stability. While reciprocal* exchange maintains hierarchies within and between societies, gift cycles involving spiritual beings demand transfers to the poor that buffer the effects of inequality.

* Mauss shows that supernatural elements of gift and commercial transactions persist in complex societies. He provides a model for investigating the implicit motivations and meanings embedded in economic behavior everywhere.

Other Ideas

In *The Gift*, Marcel Mauss proposes that local variants of the Pacific Polynesian* and Melanesian* concept of *mana** explain how archaic cultures* infuse gifts with religious, spiritual, and magical forces. In *A General Theory of Magic*, a 1904 publication written with the historian and sociologist Henri Hubert,* Mauss explains that these concepts refer to a spiritual force that pervades the universe.[1] Throughout the southern Pacific, Africa, Asia, the Americas, and the Middle East, archaic societies attribute power and advantages to the *mana* attached to objects and possessions, and, through them, to people. To illustrate the *mana*-like qualities of gifts, Mauss describes the Maori*—indigenous New Zealand—concept of *hau*,* or the power of a class of gifts that carries them back to their place of origin. Where political and legal structures, honor, and concern for social status fail, the spirit of the gift itself ensures that it will continue to circulate.[2]

Mauss draws an analogy between these beliefs and alms (charitable gifts) as a form of gift exchange with the spirits, a topic covered in "Essai sur la Nature et la Fonction du Sacrifice," his 1898 work with Henri Hubert on the role of sacrifice in ancient religions.[3] Just as sacrificial offerings are given to the spirits in recognition of their gifts to humans and as a way to attract future benefits, through alms to the poor the better-off demonstrate awareness of their place in the cycle of exchange that is the source of their wealth and good fortune. Mauss cites beliefs about almsgiving as a principle of justice and obligation under the threat of divine retribution in Christianity and Islam and among the Hausa (an ethnic Sub-Saharan people) of the northeast African nation of Sudan, the ancient Semites and Hindus, and Arab cultures.

The spiritual grease for the wheels of exchange furnished by concepts such as *mana* and *hau*, as well as their relation to alms, supports Mauss's principal ideas about the obligatory nature of gift cycles. Mauss argues that rich members of industrialized societies should be reminded of their custodial role vis-à-vis the poor. The blessing of overabundance demands to be acknowledged through redistribution.

> *"Thus [Maori gifts] contain within them that force, in cases where the law, particularly the obligation to reciprocate, may fail to be observed."*
> —— Marcel Mauss, *The Gift: The Form and Reason for Exchange in Archaic Societies*

Exploring the Ideas

Mauss explains that gifts are alive; they carry something of the person or people who held them previously; and they insist on continued movement. To illustrate, he analyzes the Maori concept of *hau* that pertains primarily to objects known as *taonga*, gifts passed along maternal lines such as mats, decorations, and talismans. These are defined as fixed property linked to its place of origin, in contrast to *oloa* or movable objects such as tools. While *taonga* items may be traded for other things such as food in ordinary transactions, when given as gifts, *hau* demands that they be returned on pain of serious, potentially mortal, harm to the holder.

The *taonga* "is animated by the *hau* of its forest, its native heath and soil."[4] Moreover, the *taonga* carries some part of the person who gives it:"The *taonga* or its *hau* ... is attached to this chain of users until these give back ... by way of feasts, festivals, and presents, the equivalent or something of even greater value. This in turn will give the donors authority and power over the first donor, who has become the last recipient. This is the key idea that in Samoa and New Zealand seems to dominate the obligatory circulation of wealth, tribute, and gifts."[5]

Mauss suggests that for many simple societies gifts *are living things*, not a metaphor for them. Referring to ancient Hindu laws, he explains:"The land, the food, and all that one gives are, moreover, personified: they are living creatures with whom one enters into a dialogue, and who share in the contract. They seek to be given away."[6]

Similarly, in Germany and France contracts involving sales and loans are accompanied by a personal object of little value that is "infused with the individuality of the donor" and returned upon completion of the deal.[7] This tradition derives from the earlier practice of cutting a pledge object in two for the contracting parties to keep and by which they exerted power over one another.

These examples illustrate Mauss's point that the spiritual quality of gifts supplies what legal strictures cannot: a psychological motivation rooted in supernatural awe.

Overlooked

The idea that mystical forces infuse the world around us, including gifts, has not been received with the same enthusiasm as Mauss's main framework for analyzing the legal and cultural systems behind reciprocal* exchange. One reason is that evidence for analogous concepts to *mana* and *hau* is relatively scarce in *The Gift*.[8] Another reason is that Western society's scientific mindset and monotheistic religions—faith in a single god—are contrary to the idea of a world enchanted by supernatural forces. This world view is consistent with utilitarianism,* a philosophical theory founded by the British philosopher Jeremy Bentham* and strongly associated with the philosopher John Stuart Mill's* writings on the central importance of individual potential and responsibility. Utilitarianism takes for granted an individualistic human nature that drives people to make rational* choices based on utility*—that is, costs and benefits are weighed and decisions are made on the practical consequence of that choice. Unless there is interference by society or the state, individual actions add up to growth and opportunity for the benefit of all.[9]

Durkheim* and Mauss rejected utilitarianism in favor of a focus on social forces. Their approach makes it possible to see that cultures define utility and rationality in different ways, including ones that account for social and spiritual relationships. Since then the influence of utilitarianism has ebbed and flowed through popular culture and political philosophy. It has found new life in the economic school of neoliberalism (an economic philosophy of the late twentieth and early twenty-first centuries that revives nineteenth-century liberalism's* emphasis on economic growth through free-market principles and law-based governance free of interference in individual liberties) and in new forms of social Darwinism (the use of evolutionary theory to explain the different traits and fortunes of individuals or groups of people as a consequence of their biological inferiority or superiority). These ideas are based on assumptions of human nature as definable by self-interest, and the naturalness of utilitarian market* exchange— that the economic marketplace, which operates according to the exercise of selfishness, is somehow natural.

While Mauss's insights into the mystical elements of reciprocal exchange may be considered secondary to his principal arguments, they have not been entirely overlooked. Scholars and critics examine why wealthy individuals give to charity and spend large sums on art and other non-utilitarian possessions, as Mauss notes. They question whether conspicuous consumption concerns something more than class-climbing in the nineteenth-century sense described by the US sociologist and economist Thorstein Veblen.*[10] Researchers have identified spiritual or magical beliefs in organ donation, because biological gifts are often seen as alive with the donor's personhood*—and so impose obligations on recipients and their families.[11]

---

1. Marcel Mauss and Henri Hubert, *A General Theory of Magic* (London: Routledge, 2001).
2. Marcel Mauss, *The Gift: The Form and Reason for Exchange in Archaic Societies* (London: Routledge, 1990), 8–13.
3. Marcel Mauss and Henri Hubert, "Essai sur la Nature et la Fonction du Sacrifice," *L'Année Sociologique* (1897–8): 29–138.
4. Mauss, *The Gift*, 11–12.
5. Mauss, *The Gift*, 12.
6. Mauss, *The Gift*, 56.
7. Mauss, *The Gift*, 62.
8. Seth Leacock, "The Ethnological Theory of Marcel Mauss," *American Anthropologist* 56 (1954): 63–4.
9. Marshall Sahlins, *The Western Illusion of Human Nature: With Reflections on the Long History of Hierarchy, Equality and the Sublimation of Anarchy in the West, and Comparative Notes on Other Conceptions of the Human Condition* (Chicago: Prickly Paradigm Press, 2008).
10. Thorstein Veblen, *The Theory of the Leisure Class: An Economic Study of the Evolution of Institutions* (New York: MacMillan, 1899).
11. Lesley A. Sharp, "Commodified Kin: Death, Mourning, and Competing Claims on the Bodies of Organ Donors in the United States," *American Anthropologist* 103, no. 1 (2001): 112–33.

ACHIEVEMENT

KEY POINTS

* Mauss shows that the binding obligations inherent in gift cycles project social relationships into the future. He extends the principle that economic transactions are socially regulated and culturally meaningful from societies without money to those that run on market* principles (with the economic exchange of goods based on established calculated values).

* The analysis brings together the ethnographic* research of other scholars with Mauss's own interpretations of ancient laws and literature, which he read in the original languages.

* Mauss convincingly draws parallels between gifts and commercial transactions in existing and historical archaic societies.* He is less successful with regard to implications for industrialized societies due to a scarcity of relevant empirical data.

Assessing the Argument

Marcel Mauss's comparison of reciprocal* exchange systems in small societies in *The Gift* shows how combined, collective representations* (shared beliefs and understandings) and social institutions* (formalized relationships or activities such as retirement or marriage) define social interaction and channel human behavior in specific ways. In addition to legal frameworks, the moral and mystical baggage attached to gifts ensures that they will be returned or passed on, often with increase and according to a predetermined time frame. Trade* and barter* occur alongside these "systems of total prestation" (that is, customary payment). Goods such as blankets, fish, yams, and copper objects carry fixed values in relation to each other, and repayment can involve a delay. In some cases there is currency* such as shells, pieces of metal, and coins belonging to individuals or clans.* In all of these societies there are concepts of purchasing power, debt, and credit, just as there are in modern societies.[1]

Mauss argues that the reverse is also true: archaic gift cycles persist in modern market economies.* This is evident in laws, literature, and the obligation to return invitations. It explains gambling and other exchanges involving honor and theoretically voluntary, but obligatory, payment, and the fact that "Charity is still wounding for him who has accepted it."[2]

However, redistribution now occurs through taxes and legislative processes, which interrupt the cycle of exchange that puts people's honor at stake. While anonymous transactions are not simply the outcome of individual rational* choices separate from cultural values, it is difficult to assess the symbolic and social meaning of spending behavior. Likewise, more evidence is needed to demonstrate that a higher proportion of gift versus commercial exchanges correlates with a higher level of social cohesion.

These limitations mean that Mauss can only offer recommendations for the modern world. He suggests combining lessons from archaic societies with individuality, market principles, and the will to work. In this way, complex societies can prevent the exploitation of the poor, more fully compensate laborers through social protections, and acknowledge that it is never possible or even desirable to completely fulfill an obligation.[3]

Achievement in Context

Mauss was not the first to examine economic exchange as a socially ordered phenomenon governed by cultural beliefs or collective representations. In *The Philosophy of Money* in 1907 the German philosopher and sociologist* Georg Simmel* analyzed economic systems in relation to social interaction and symbolic meanings, and showed that the value of things is changeable and socially constructed.[4] *The Protestant Ethic and the Spirit of Capitalism*, pioneering sociologist Max Weber's* 1904–5 analysis of the rise of capitalism* in Europe, traced connections between religious beliefs, economic organization, and individual behavior;[5] capitalism is the economic and social model, founded on the private ownership of industry and business, dominant in the West (and increasingly throughout the Western world) today.

Mauss's work was distinctive in its focus on archaic societies across great spans of time and space. Mauss shifted the focus on the social and cultural shaping of economic behavior to transactions that occur in the absence of money and under the guise of gifts. *The Gift* took the study of total social phenomena to a different level.

The essay was first published in 1923–4 in French in the journal *L'Année Sociologique*,* and was not translated into English until 30 years later. The lack of a translation and the essay's publication in a scholarly journal limited its accessibility outside the circle of intellectuals capable of reading multiple European languages. These same readers would have been familiar with the Durkheimian* school of sociology as well as the work of Simmel and Weber.

Within these limits, *The Gift* was influential from the start. In addition to exploring a unique theme through a novel approach, the essay appeared after a long lull in publication of *L'Année Sociologique* and was written by one of Durkheim's successors. The book's contribution to the development of British structural-functionalism* was ensured through scholars whose ethnographic writings were its source material, including A. R. Radcliffe-Brown* and Bronislaw Malinowski.*

Although the anthropologist* Raymond Firth,* a scholar of indigenous New Zealand cultures, disputed the way Mauss interpreted the data he had collected among the Maori,* the book's influence was not affected by concerns over the quality of the evidence used.[6] Those concerns emerged decades later, when scholars began to rethink the premises behind fieldwork conducted by previous generations of researchers. The circumstances framing ethnographic encounters and the attitudes and abilities of researchers came under fire, bringing a reevaluation of the validity of their findings.

Limitations

Mauss's analysis of gift exchange as a social institution underpinned by a bundle of collective representations concerning obligation, honor, and, in at least some cases, supernatural forces, has passed the test of time. Although some of its ideas have been cast aside, the book's impact has not been limited by the subject matter, theoretical approach, or linkage to a single time or place. Even the whole set of nomadic foraging* (hunter-gatherer) societies unknown to Mauss show some of the characteristics and dynamics he identified in relation to settled foragers of the Northwest Coast of North America and village-based agriculturalists studied by ethnographers throughout the world in the late nineteenth and early twentieth centuries.

The text has not been severely challenged since its publication. Even after social evolutionary* theory (founded on the idea that societies progress through a fixed series of stages of ever-increasing technological, social, and intellectual perfection) and structural-functionalism (a theory that focuses on the ways in which societies are structured and in which their internal parts are integrated with one another) lost favor along with the method of comparative analysis,* The Gift remained a foundational text across many disciplines. Mauss's partial acceptance of the prevalent evolutionary doctrines of his time did not fundamentally distort his analysis. His comparative method was thorough and well grounded in a comprehensive analysis of beliefs and practices in context, in contrast to the opportunistic use of ethnographic research on the part of evolutionists intent upon arranging social facts in a predetermined classificatory scheme.

Mauss and Durkheim have been criticized for their alleged

failure to consider individuals and social change. However, although they focused on collective representations and social institutions, they also thought about individual personhood* and the relationship between social norms and individual belief and action. They had a theory of change that is implicit in Mauss's analysis of shifts in systems of gift exchange in step with changes in politico-economic organization.[7]

The Gift is relevant not only to anthropology and sociology but disciplines across the humanities and social sciences, including linguistics, economics, history, philosophy, and political science. The book continues to provide a basis for analyzing past and present behavior and social norms. It transmits ethnographic portraits of an earlier age that might otherwise be forgotten.

---

1. Marcel Mauss, The Gift: The Form and Reason for Exchange in Archaic Societies (London: Routledge, 1990), 36, 100–1.

2. Mauss, The Gift, 65, 112.

3. Mary Douglas, "Foreword: No Free Gifts," in The Gift by Marcel Mauss (London: Routledge, 2000), xv.

4. Georg Simmel, The Philosophy of Money (London: Routledge, 1978).

5. Max Weber, The Protestant Ethic and the Spirit of Capitalism: The Relationships between Religion and the Economic and Social Life in Modern Culture (New York: Charles Scribner's Sons, 1958).

6. Raymond Firth, Primitive Economics of the New Zealand Maori (London: Routledge, 1929).

7. Douglas, "Foreword: No Free Gifts"; Seth Leacock, "The Ethnological Theory of Marcel Mauss," American Anthropologist 56 (1954): 58–71.

PLACE IN THE AUTHOR'S WORK

KEY POINTS

* Marcel Mauss's teaching, writing, and political engagement were unified by a focus on the social norms, shared beliefs, and legal structures that direct human interaction and influence social solidarity.*

* *The Gift* exemplifies Mauss's approach: the essay integrates earlier ethnological* comparisons (comparisons drawn from the study of ethnographic material) and sociological* theories with reflections on the positive and negative sides of modern civilization.

* *The Gift* was Mauss's last major comparative analysis* and his most significant scholarly contribution. His later work remained consistent with its premises and approach.

Positioning

The foundational anthropologist* Claude Lévi-Strauss* calls *The Gift* Marcel Mauss's "masterpiece" and "most deservedly famous" publication;[1] the US anthropologist Walter Goldschmidt* says it is Mauss's "most important noncollaborative effort."[2] The book is emblematic of the transition between nineteenth-century positivism and twentieth-century social anthropology ushered in by Émile Durkheim* and his associates in the years before World War I.* Positivism is a scientific system established by the French philosopher Auguste Comte to unify disciplines from mathematics to sociology through the same basic principles and standards of evidence.

Throughout his career, Mauss collaborated frequently, taught and learned as a lifelong student, and mixed intellectual and political writing. Mauss preferred to concentrate on "his materials" as opposed to engaging in theoretical debates or defending cherished dogma. He built bridges with other scholars, was not stopped by disciplinary boundaries, and avoided clashes by sticking to Durkheim's positivist emphasis on empirical (that is, verifiable) evidence. The French anthropologist Maurice Leenhardt* sums up Mauss's contribution:"Few books, articles dispersed everywhere, an enormous influence."[3]

In addition to *The Gift*, Mauss's body of work includes his studies on magic, religion, money, mourning customs, suicide, Bolshevism* (the political movement on which the Soviet Union* was originally founded) and violence. For the journal *L'Année Sociologigue** Mauss contributed short pieces and book reviews, and edited numerous unfinished works by Durkheim and other scholars. In addition, collections of Mauss's writings on methodology, sociology, and politics were published in his final years and after his death in 1950.[4]

Mauss's productivity diminished after publication of *The Gift*, due to the deaths of many of his closest associates during World War I* and the political turbulence of the interwar period. Mauss diverted his energies to political activism and institutional development in the French university system. He left several unfinished manuscripts on topics including Bolshevism, prayer, the nation, and technology.[5]

Many of the topics and empirical evidence discussed in *The*

Gift appear in Mauss's previous writings on religion, magic, and the social organization of seasonal productive activity. Mauss's political activism trained his attention on legal systems and the political dimensions of exchange. Although he valued the comparative method, Mauss remained committed throughout his career to the view that social phenomena must be studied in their entire context. In sum, the wide range of his interests matched Mauss's lifelong goal of understanding societies in themselves, in relation to one another, and over time.

> *"In this concrete observation of social life lies the means of discovering new facts, which we are only beginning dimly to perceive. In our opinion, nothing is more urgent or more fruitful than this study of total social facts."*
> —— Marcel Mauss, *The Gift: The Form and Reason for Exchange in Archaic Societies*

Integration

Claude Lévi-Strauss explains that Mauss was ahead of his time in realizing that "the mental and the social are one and the same."[6] In 1926, Mauss reported on cultural beliefs that result in mortal harm to individuals, reflecting his appreciation of the society-body-mind nexus—that is, the whole formed by the combination of these things.[7] A 1934 paper,"Les Techniques du Corps," examined the imprinting of cultural beliefs on small children through the management of bodily processes.[8] The American anthropologist Ruth Benedict's* comparative analysis of indigenous* populations in Melanesia,* New Mexico, and the Northwest Coast of North America appeared the same year. Together the two scholars helped develop an emerging discipline concerned with culture* and personality, mental ability, and psychological distress.[9]

At the same time, in some respects Mauss remained set in his ways. While he avoided using words such as "primitive" or "inferior," he nevertheless grouped societies according to their place on an evolutionary* progression throughout his career. In a 1938 lecture, Mauss discussed the evolution of individuality through the same ordering of ethnographic and historical sources presented in *The Gift*.[10]

The relationship between individuality on the one hand, and the ways in which economic behavior is constrained by non-economic institutions, social justice, and solidarity on the other, was a constant theme running through Mauss's work. In *The Gift*, Mauss explains that societies at a middle stage of social evolution* learned how to institutionalize gift relationships as a way to protect against shortages and avoid violence. This took the uncertainty and risk out of intergroup encounters typical of earlier stages of human history, in which the idea of individual personhood* barely existed.[11]

In middle-stage societies, trading for personal reasons arises alongside systems of obligation that channel prestige, honor, and exchange goods towards group leaders. In more advanced societies, individuality flourishes because money distances exchange relationships from their social and moral context. Traces of archaic exchange remain in forms such as charitable giving, worker consciousness of the inadequacy of wages as compensation for labor, and bank-breaking outlays of cash for ceremonial feasts. Mauss's scholarly and political interests come together in his view that these surviving elements of reciprocity* should be cultivated in order to promote justice, economic growth, and peace.

Significance

Mauss's most significant intellectual legacy is, without a doubt, *The Gift*. The book has been required reading for anthropology students for generations. It has inspired other comparative analyses and an enormous amount of research on reciprocity and exchange relationships. Although the book's social evolutionary premises have been abandoned and the comparative method severely challenged since its publication, Mauss's insights into collective representations* and the interrelationships among social, economic, political, and religious institutions* have remained compelling.

The book is a landmark text and a testament to Mauss's knowledge, linguistic abilities, and exacting scholarship. However, the book alone is not the basis for its author's reputation. Mauss was a political activist, a contributor to and editor of political and academic publications, the co-founder of academic institutes, and a teacher and lecturer. He shared his ideas with other scholars, coauthored many publications, and strengthened Durkheim's influence on the human sciences.

Although Durkheim left an enormous imprint on Mauss's thinking, which the latter gratefully acknowledged, Mauss's work took its own path. Unlike Durkheim, Mauss immersed himself in the political struggles of his time and drew connections to his academic work. Nonetheless the two are often criticized together for ignoring individuals in favor of disembodied social facts and presuming a tight, stable fit between collective representations and social institutions. The British scholar Mary Douglas,* however, says that Durkheim and Mauss both considered the role of individual minds in generating and maintaining collective representations, and were not uninterested in change. For example, the line of argumentation in *The Gift* reflects an underlying theory of social change by which economic transactions shift from gift to contract.[12]

Although grounded in his uncle's sociological tradition, Mauss's reputation and impact derive from his own particular focus and findings. *The Gift* exemplifies Mauss's conviction that comparison based on reliable, detailed, contextualized data about "total social facts" is the key to understanding human societies and individual behavior.

---

1. Seth Leacock, "The Ethnological Theory of Marcel Mauss," *American Anthropologist* 56 (1954): 65; Marcel Fournier, *Marcel Mauss: A Biography* (Princeton, NJ: Princeton University Press, 2005), 1.

2. Walter Goldschmidt, "Untitled Review of *The Gift* by Marcel Mauss," *American Anthropologist* 57, no. 6 (1955): 1299.

3. Fournier, *Marcel Mauss*, 4.

4. Marcel Mauss, *Manuel d'Ethnographie* (Paris: Payot, 1947); Marcel Mauss, *Sociologie et Anthropologie* (Paris: Presses Universaires de France, 1950).

5. Fournier, *Marcel Mauss*; Goldschmidt, "Untitled Review"; Leacock, "The Ethnological Theory."

6. Claude Lévi-Strauss, *Introduction to the Work of Marcel Mauss* (London: Routledge and Kegan

Paul, 1987), 21.

7. Marcel Mauss "Effet Physique chez l'Individu de l'Idée de Mort Suggérée par la Collectivité," *Journal de Psychologie Normale et Pathologique* XXIII, no. 6 (1926): 653–9.

8. Marcel Mauss, "Les Techniques du Corps," *Journal de Psychologie Normale et Pathologique* XXXII, nos 3–4 (1934): 271–93.

9. Lévi-Strauss, *Introduction*, 3–8, 11–13.

10. Marcel Mauss, "Une Catégorie de l'Esprit Humain," *Journal of the Royal Anthropological Institute* XLVIII, no. 2 (1938): 263–81; Leacock, "The Ethnological Theory," 69–70.

11. Marcel Mauss, *The Gift: The Form and Reason for Exchange in Archaic Societies* (London: Routledge, 1990).

12. Mary Douglas, "Foreword: No Free Gifts," in *The Gift* by Marcel Mauss (London: Routledge, 2000).

SECTION 3
IMPACT

THE FIRST RESPONSES

KEY POINTS

* *The Gift* has been criticized mainly for overstating the continuity among concepts and practices across cultures. Critics also argue that the book's evolutionary framework ties it and its author more to the past than the future of anthropology* and sociology.*

* Mauss's supporters argue that his analysis in *The Gift* was methodologically sound and empirically accurate (that is, founded on verifiable evidence). They point out that his other work on mind-body connections and the interrelated social and biological spheres of human existence was ahead of its time.

* The 30-year time lag before translation into English was a major factor in the book's reception. By the 1950s, social evolutionism* and comparative analysis* had fallen out of favor in anthropology, leading to *The Gift* being criticized on both accounts.

Criticism

Most of the scholars cited by Marcel Mauss in *The Gift*, including Bronislaw Malinowski* and Franz Boas,* reacted positively to the book.[1] The anthropologist Raymond Firth,* an expert on indigenous New Zealand culture, however, questioned the originality of the analysis and disputed Mauss's interpretation of Maori* customs and concepts.[2]

After the author's death and the book's publication in English in 1954, *The Gift* was criticized by a generation of anthropologists who were wary of the search for general laws, the progressive logic of evolutionism, and the method of comparative analysis. They argued that Mauss overemphasized similarities in institutions* across cultures* and ignored or downplayed differences, possibly as a result of his lack of fieldwork experience.[3] More, they criticized Mauss for disapproving of the English anthropologist J. G. Frazer* for presuming the universality of totemism* (the practice of infusing a neutral object with sacredness as the symbol for a group of people) without evidence, while extending terms such as *potlatch** and *mana** (a spiritual force potentially attached to objects) to the institutions of societies where parallel, local concepts were lacking.[4] *Potlatch* was a ceremonial feast practiced by Native American populations in Northwest North America that includes gifts to the guests; it was a means for the competitive display of wealth and prestige that even included the destruction of objects.

Even though Mauss discussed self-aggrandizement and the desire to belittle rivals, critics argued that he underplayed negative elements because they complicated the larger message that reciprocity* is necessary for social cohesion. Walter Goldschmidt* noted that his own studies of societies in Mauss's middle-range category revealed very clearly the greed, unscrupulousness, and "cold reasoning" involved in reciprocal exchange relationships.[5]

Finally, the knowledge that the institutions of simple societies are not just precursors to those of complex societies has called into question the value of evolutionary stages as a useful tool for investigating and interpreting human societies. This had led many critics to dismiss Mauss's conclusions about how to improve human interaction in modern societies by expanding upon what's left of surviving forms of reciprocity.

> "The sense of work in common, as a team, the conviction that collaboration is a force against isolation, against the pretentious search for originality, may be what characterizes my scientific career, even more now perhaps than before."
> ——Marcel Mauss, "L'Oeuvre de Mauss par lui-même"

Responses

On the one hand, Mauss oriented his work according to a social evolutionary framework throughout his career, as seen in his 1938 publication on the evolution of autonomous individuality.[6] On the other hand, although he and Émile Durkheim* wrote in 1901 that, once scientifically described, social facts became simply data for comparative analysis, Mauss taught all his life that contextualization (considering information in its social and environmental context) is the necessary basis of well-founded cross-cultural knowledge.[7] He did not take comparison lightly. To illustrate, in *The Gift*, he states that it would be "too easy and too dangerous" to speculate about the migration or independent origin of customs. "For the time being, it must suffice to show the nature and very widespread diffusion of what is a legal theme. Let others write its history, if they can."[8]

In spite of having applied ideas from his study of gift exchange to European economies with the goal of making modern societies less impersonal and individualistic, in 1930 Mauss was wary of ethical conclusions drawn from ethnological comparisons. When it came to the idea of the absorption of all cultures into a global monoculture, Mauss "cautioned against applying value judgments to this trend, since it, as well as 'progress,' cannot be shown to lead necessarily to good or to happiness."[9] While unflagging in his moral and institutional support for members of the Collège de Sociologie, which met in Paris from 1937 to 1939—especially the French thinkers Georges Bataille* and Roger Caillois*—Mauss did not approve of the way they applied his ideas from *The Gift* to their analysis of the sacred* in modern society.[10]

These critical responses to *The Gift* may partly explain why the book was Mauss's last large comparative analysis. After *The Gift* his attention shifted to topics such as psychological phenomena and political questions explored through a sociological perspective. None of this subsequent scholarship led Mauss to alter the original version of *The Gift*.

Conflict and Consensus

The originality of Mauss's work has been questioned—but, as he wrote in 1930, originality did not really interest him.[11] He was more concerned with collaboration, the analysis of concrete data, and cross-disciplinary thinking. Mauss practiced what he preached about reciprocity: he was kind, generous, and committed to sharing ideas and materials with others. As a result he published fewer manuscripts than he might have done, and *The Gift* stands out as one of the few he wrote alone.

There is no disagreement about Mauss's contribution to

anthropological understanding of the ways that economic systems are embedded in broader social systems that encompass politics, kinship,* and religion. For instance, the 1940 work of the influential British anthropologist E. E. Evans-Pritchard,* who wrote the introduction to *The Gift*'s 1954 translation, described marriage payments among the Nuer people of southern Sudan as a "strand in the total circulation of cattle, and wives, and children, and men: every single relationship had its substantiation in a gift."[12]

As the "father of French ethnography,"* Mauss left an undisputed mark on the practice of anthropological research.[13] Although he did not have personal experience and saw fieldwork in terms of a brief expedition as opposed to long-term immersion, Mauss taught a precise, thorough method of data collection.[14] This is evident in the lectures he gave at the Institut d'Ethnologie from 1926 to 1939, and the fieldwork of students such as the sociologist Henri Lévy-Bruhl.*[15]

Mauss's work has inspired generations of those conducting research in the field to map out reciprocal transfers as a point of access to interlinked sociopolitical institutions.[16] In *Elementary Forms of Kinship*, Claude Lévi-Strauss* describes transfers of men, women, and children as gifts in a network of mutual obligation and symbolic meaning. In other words, kinship* relations emerge through an integrated communication/exchange system.[17]

After the 1950s, scholars increasingly criticized the presumed objectivity and search for general laws embraced by Mauss and other followers of Durkheim. World events of the 1960s and 1970s contributed to a rethinking of the sources of knowledge, and these developments cast doubt on the validity of data gathered by earlier fieldworkers not trained to be critically aware of their own cultural biases.

1. Marcel Fournier, *Marcel Mauss: A Biography* (Princeton, NJ: Princeton University Press, 2005), 244.

2. Firth argued that *hau* did not attach any element of the giver's personhood to the gift, although it did give the gift a life force. Barth points out that evidence from India supports Mauss's idea that something like *hau* explains the personhood carried by gifts in societies around the world. Fredrik Barth et al., *One Discipline, Four Ways: British, German, French, and American Anthropology* (Chicago: University of Chicago Press, 2005), 189; Raymond Firth, *Primitive Economics of the New Zealand Maori* (London: Routledge, 1929).

3. Seth Leacock, "The Ethnological Theory of Marcel Mauss," *American Anthropologist* 56 (1954): 59–60; Walter Goldschmidt, "Untitled Review of *The Gift* by Marcel Mauss," *American Anthropologist* 57, no. 6 (1955): 1299.

4. Leacock, "The Ethnological Theory," 63.

5. Goldschmidt, "Untitled Review," 1300.

6. Leacock, "The Ethnological Theory," 70.

7. Leacock, "The Ethnological Theory," 67.

8. Marcel Mauss, *The Gift: The Form and Reason for Exchange in Archaic Societies* (London: Routledge, 1990), 98.

9. Leacock, "The Ethnological Theory," 64.

10. Fournier, *Marcel Mauss*, 327.

11. Marcel Mauss, "L'œuvre de Mauss par Lui-Même." *Revue Française de Sociologie* 20, nos 20–21 (1979): 209.

12. Mary Douglas, "Foreword: No Free Gifts," in *The Gift* by Marcel Mauss (London: Routledge, 2000), xv.

13. Georges Condominas, "Marcel Mauss, Père de l'ethnographie française," *Critique* 28, no. 297 (1972): 118–39.

14. Barth et al., *One Discipline, Four Ways*, 159.

15. Marcel Mauss, *Manuel d'ethnographie* (Paris: Payot, 1947).

16. Douglas, "Foreword: No Free Gifts," xii–xiii.

17. Claude Lévi-Strauss, *The Elementary Structures of Kinship* (Boston: Beacon Press, 1969); Douglas, "Foreword: No Free Gifts," xv.

THE EVOLVING DEBATE

KEY POINTS

* Mauss has shown that exchanges that may seem invisible or inconsequential are central to human relationships and socioeconomic systems. This insight continues to inspire research on the link between open-ended reciprocity* and social cohesion in simple and complex societies.

* The book and the resulting critical dialogue has stimulated developments in the study of individual agency* (the capacity to act) in relation to social-structural constraints, comparative economic and political systems, and the production of knowledge.

* The book has had a mixed impact. It is a model of empirical richness and original insight into a complex phenomenon, but its evolutionary assumptions and insufficient attention to variability ground it in an earlier era and indicate hazards to avoid.

Uses and Problems

Marcel Mauss's most influential work, *The Gift* was part of an intellectual current that arose in France in opposition to British philosophy's utilitarian* theories of the eighteenth and nineteenth centuries, oriented toward the individual. Along with Émile Durkheim* and the rest of the group of scholars united around the journal *L'Année Sociologique*,* Mauss sought to understand how society shaped the thoughts and behavior of individuals. These scholars explored the interaction between cultural beliefs and social institutions* and its connection to social solidarity.* Mauss contributed by showing how reciprocal exchange creates binding social relationships that endure over time because gifts must be returned after a delay.

This current soon merged with the British theoretical approach of structural-functionalism,* which shared the basic assumption that the components of society work together to maintain stability and equilibrium. French structuralist* approaches under Claude Lévi-Strauss* were more specifically concentrated on explaining the way elements within myths, rituals, and stories were organized, how they related to one another, and what they expressed about culture and thought. All forms of structuralism came under fire in the 1960s and 1970s, as scholars questioned the totalizing force of collective representations* (shared beliefs and understandings), which they saw as too fixed and far removed from the minds of individuals acting in society.[1]

The focus shifted to discord and cultural dynamism. Symbolic or "interpretive" anthropologists led by Victor Turner* and Clifford Geertz,* known for their work in Africa and Indonesia respectively, explored myths, rituals, and symbols in motion through concrete situations; they examined social action, gaps and reversals in structure, and how meaning is constructed and embodied by individuals. The French sociologist Pierre Bourdieu* focused on power and its different vehicles such as social and symbolic capital, or forms of wealth such as reputation or control over knowledge that confer power similarly to financial assets. Bourdieu reintroduced the classical concept of habitus*—the embodiment of social and cultural conditions—that Mauss had explored in his 1934 work on the imprinting of social constructs on the body in childhood:"Les Techniques du Corps."[2] The linking of lived experience, inequalities of power, and language and culture* generated an enduring focus in social science on the ways in which sociocultural forces constrain individual agency (or the freedom and resources necessary for knowing and realizing one's own will).[3]

> "For the sheer range and imagination of his writings, which are nonetheless still rooted in the fairly well-delineated model drawn up by his uncle, Mauss has few peers."
> —— Fredrik Barth,* One Discipline, Four Ways: British, German, French, and American Anthropology

Schools of Thought

The interpretive, reflexive turn away from structuralism and functionalism occurred at the same time as troubling details emerged concerning the fieldwork conducted during the first half of the twentieth century. Clifford Geertz described how Malinowski's* diary revealed a physical and psychological detachment and cold, disdainful opinion of the "natives" expressed in coarse language.[4] The anthropologist Margaret Mead's* fieldwork in New Guinea was limited by an injured ankle and her lack of proficiency in indigenous* languages. These problems undermine her conclusions about different gender systems across three societies, which seem also to have been shaped by her personal life and professional agenda.[5] Lévi-Strauss likewise conducted brief expedition-type field visits and had very little knowledge of indigenous languages, as is evident from his own descriptions of ethnographic* research.

Ethnographers responded by turning their critical eye inward, upon their own preconceptions and social position and the larger power structures that privilege the wealthy and educated over their informants. The fact that anthropologists are their own research instruments and therefore cannot help but affect the field of observation and quality of the data has had positive effects on scholarship. On the other hand, it has cast doubt on the validity of previous ethnographic accounts and the comparative spirit of earlier scholars, including Mauss.

Mauss's ideas emerged during the formative phase of modern sociology* and consequently have influenced work across the humanities and social sciences. Mauss was an independent thinker but also a great collaborator who believed in intellectual reciprocity. It is fitting that his ideas did not give rise to specific schools of thought but rather have been influential in a variety of understated and at times indirect ways.

In Current Scholarship

The Gift continues to inspire scholarship, literature, and social and political debate, particularly among French writers. Mauss's (and Durkheim's) demonstration of the lack of an intrinsic connection between the properties of sacred*—spiritually important—objects and the meanings assigned to them converged, in time, with the influential Swiss linguist Ferdinand de Saussure's* teachings on language. This shared insight had far-reaching consequences for structuralist approaches to the study of language and myth led by Lévi-Strauss, and poststructuralist* work pioneered by the psychoanalyst Jacques Lacan* in psychology, linguistics, and literature;[6] poststructuralist theory rejected structuralist ideas, particularly the idea that it was possible to arrive at any objective truth in the course of analysis. The philosopher Paul Ricoeur's* concept of "the economy of the gift," among other ideas, drew directly from Mauss.[7] Other French scholars who have taken inspiration from Mauss's work on exchange and human relationships include the philosophers Jean-Luc Marion,* Maurice Godelier,* and Jacques Derrida* (a thinker noted for an approach to the analysis of symbol and meaning known as "deconstructionism").[8]

The Gift has also had a lasting impact on the sociology and anthropology* of economic and political systems, as in the German sociologist Helmuth Berking's* Sociology of Giving.[9] In part through the Hungarian American thinker Karl Polanyi's* influential work on the social history of Europe, Mauss's ideas reached a receptive audience of American scholars and supported their approach to and interest in economic anthropology.[10] Recent work in this area includes studies on the economics and cultural value of creativity in commercial society by the American writer Lewis Hyde;* the history of formal rules for gift-giving by the American writer and legal scholar Richard Hyland;* and gift exchange in the

industrial era by the American historian Harry Liebersohn.*[11]
Finally, Mauss's call to combine political and scholarly writing
has been taken up by scholars interested in contemporary social
policy such as Alan Schrift.*[12] The anti-utilitarian "Mouvement Anti-
Utilitariste dans les Sciences Sociales" (MAUSS), founded in 1981
by the French thinkers Alain Caillé* and Gérald Berthoud,* focuses
on economic, ethical, and environmental crises including income
insecurity, a topic Mauss touches upon in his conclusion to *The
Gift*.[13] Caillé remains the editor of the anti-utilitarian journal *Revue
du MAUSS*. The name in the title, an acronym for the *Mouvement*,
honors Mauss's lasting influence on French sociology.

---

1. Mary Douglas, "Foreword: No Free Gifts," in *The Gift* by Marcel Mauss (London: Routledge, 2000); Seth Leacock, "The Ethnological Theory of Marcel Mauss," *American Anthropologist* 56 (1954): 58–71.

2. Marcel Mauss, "Les Techniques du Corps," *Journal de Psychologie Normale et Pathologique* XXXII, nos 3–4 (1934): 271–93.

3. Pierre Bourdieu, *Outline of a Theory of Practice* (Cambridge: Cambridge University Press, 1977); Clifford Geertz, "From the Native's Point of View," in *Local Knowledge* by Clifford Geertz (New York: Basic Books, 1983), 54–70; Victor Turner, *Dramas, Fields, and Metaphors: Symbolic Action in Human Society* (Ithaca, NY: Cornell University Press, 1974); Victor Turner, *The Ritual Process: Structure and Anti-Stucture* (Chicago: Aldine, 1969).

4. Geertz, "From the Native's Point of View," 54–5.

5. Lise M. Dobrin and Ira Bashkow, "'Arapesh Warfare': Reo Fortune's Veiled Critique of Margaret Mead's Sex and Temperament," *American Anthropologist* 112, no. 3 (2010): 370–83; Margaret Mead, *Sex and Temperament in Three Primitive Societies* (New York: William Morrow, 1935).

6. Ferdinand De Saussure, *Course in General Linguistics* (New York: McGraw-Hill, 1959).

7. Paul Ricoeur, *Memory, History, Forgetting* (Chicago: University of Chicago Press, 2004).

8. Jean-Luc Marion, *Being Given: Toward a Phenomenology of Givenness* (Palo Alta, CA: Stanford University Press, 2002); Maurice Godelier, *L'Enigme du Don* (Paris: Fayard, 1996); Jacques

· Derrida, *The Gift of Death* (Chicago: University of Chicago Press, 2007); Jacques Derrida, *Given Time* (Chicago: University of Chicago Press, 1992).

9. Helmuth Berking, *Sociology of Giving* (London: Sage Publications, 1999).

10. Leacock, "The Ethnological Theory," 65; Karl Polanyi, *The Great Transformation: The Political and Economic Origins of Our Time* (New York: Farrar and Rinehart, 1944).

11. Lewis Hyde, *The Gift: Imagination and the Erotic Life of Property* (New York: Vintage Books, 2008); Richard Hyland, *Gifts: A Study in Comparative Law* (Oxford: Oxford University Press, 2009); Harry Liebersohn, *The Return of the Gift: European History of a Global Idea* (New York: Cambridge University Press, 2011).

12. Alan D. Schrift (ed.), *The Logic of the Gift: Toward an Ethic of Generosity* (London: Routledge, 1997).

13. Alain Caillé, *Anthropologie du Don: Le Tiers Paradigme* (Paris: Desclée de Brouwer, 2000).

MODULE 11
IMPACT AND INFLUENCE TODAY

KEY POINTS

• *The Gift* remains a foundational text in the teaching of anthropology.* The book continues to influence scholarly interpretations of reciprocal* exchange and its relationship to social cohesiveness, peace, and well-being.

• The text remains relevant to ongoing analysis of the political and economic implications of gifts and commercial transactions for societies and individuals.

• Today, scholars have filled gaps in knowledge of economic exchange across cultures, suggesting ways for individuals and societies to strengthen social relationships, improve well-being, and avoid interpersonal and international conflict.

Position

Marcel Mauss's *The Gift* was written at a time in which Western scholars, who lived in hierarchical societies themselves, took for granted the existence of rulers and social inequalities. Critical analysis of power, conflict, and internal divisions as taken up by the sociologist and philosopher Pierre Bourdieu,* came later. Today, the blind spots in Mauss's work have been filled by others, opening the door to new readings of his conclusions and their implications for economic policy and interpersonal relationships.

Mauss's unconscious application of a conceptual framework typical of his class, gender, and historical moment to populations across the globe is evident in his consideration of women as trade goods and men as universal decision-makers.[1] The inappropriateness of this perspective has been demonstrated by the US anthropologist Annette Weiner* with regard to the Trobriand Islands and by the British anthropologist Marilyn Strathern* in relation to Melanesia.*2 The early anthropologists' blind spot is a testament to the power of unconscious assumptions to distort perceptions, for these early anthropologists overlooked glaring examples of gender interdependence and the far-reaching implications of matrilineal kinship (family relationships in the female line).

Mauss's uncritical acceptance of hierarchy is evident in his description of the transmission of both symbolic and institutional systems and inequalities through reciprocal exchange from generation to generation. He did not have the benefit of knowledge acquired decades later about classless, leaderless, gender-egalitarian societies that live by mobile gathering and hunting, or foraging.*3 Since the 1970s, around 50 such populations have been studied by anthropologists. These populations are the true champions of reciprocity. They are different from the rare form of sedentary (settled) foraging society represented by the populations of the Northwest Coast of the United States described in *The Gift*, which had leaders, social hierarchies, and stores of durable wealth.

Foraging societies practice a highly rule-based form of reciprocity, but they are also great defenders of individual autonomy (the capacity to act as an individual). Foraging populations challenge Mauss and Émile Durkheim's* assumption that individuality only emerges fully in complex modern societies. This does not make Mauss's work irrelevant. On the contrary, a revised view of reciprocity and redistribution extends the book's influence to current debates about political and economic issues and interpersonal relationships.

> "We should not take material acquisitiveness for granted. As Marcel Mauss put it, it is not something behind us, a natural condition, so much as it is before us, a moral value. Hence it is not so much an inevitability as an invention."
>
> —— Marshall Sahlins,* Apologies to Thucydides: Understanding History as Culture and Vice Versa

Interaction

Mobile foraging societies, which Marshall Sahlins* has famously called "the original affluent society," are small groups of individuals and families who live together without formal leaders.[4] They do not store food or accumulate more possessions than they can easily carry. Food is shared according to strict, elaborate rules, especially if it involves something rare. On average, women and men contribute about equal amounts of food. Foragers work fewer hours and enjoy better health than farmers.

Similarly to the villagers in Mauss's analysis, foragers benefit from reciprocity between groups because it protects against scarcity and prevents violent conflict. Within groups, reciprocity is a leveling device that keeps people humble and prevents feelings of envy. Arrogance is seen as a threat to individual autonomy and a menace that leads to violence. Failure to work or fulfill family and other obligations likewise is socially condemned.

Foraging societies present a challenge to Western assumptions about prehistory and consequently human nature. Taken-for-granted traits such as greed, hierarchy, male dominance, territoriality, aggressiveness, and stark self-interest all fall under the weight of evidence along with the harsh backdrop of short lives, constant misery, and servile submission to tyrants. This scenario is the core of utilitarian* philosophies of all kinds (that is, roughly, philosophies that equate usefulness and value), including the free-market economics that underpin today's system of capitalism* and today's version of social Darwinism[5] (the use of evolutionary theory to explain the different traits and fortunes of individuals or groups of people as a consequence of their biological inferiority or superiority), which incorporates the science of genetics.

The connection between reciprocity and reduced conflict described by Mauss has been confirmed by anthropologists who have studied the connection between warfare and intertribal marriages and other exchanges.[6] Other evidence comes from informal legal systems that bring together people in dispute in a community setting where whole families engage in reconciliation.[7] Cross-cultural exchanges create enduring relationships that help prevent international conflict. On the other hand, as Mauss has shown, gifts that cannot be returned, such as disaster relief and foreign aid, only increase the giver's status and power at the expense of the receiver's.[8]

The Continuing Debate

Mauss did not try to reconcile inequality with social solidarity.* Foraging societies show that inequality is not in the nature of things, supporting the anthropological project of exploring power and discord within societies. As we have seen, the absence of the accumulation of material goods together with enforced fairness in reciprocal exchange prevents the emergence of classes. Gender equality arises out of complementary or independent food gathering. However, the Hungarian American anthropologist Ernestine Friedl* has shown that egalitarianism suffers in the rare cases where men control the distribution of a scarce, unpredictable resource such as meat from large animals. Control over things with exchange value creates inequalities.[9] This pattern illustrates how reciprocal exchange can affect women and men differently within the same society. It also suggests that wherever one gender controls precious resources including honors and favors, there will be a higher level of inequality.

Friedl's analysis shares Mauss's premise that all reciprocal exchange is socially, economically, and politically meaningful. Exchange may involve non-monetary items or, alternatively, as in societies with money, the same resource may be used either for the benefit of the household (demonstrating what is termed "use value") or for cultivating potentially fruitful relationships outside the household ("exchange value"). Both reciprocal exchange and transactional sale-and-purchase coexist in all societies, as Mauss showed.

The implication is that solidarity is more likely to grow out of egalitarian systems of exchange, which preserve individual autonomy while maintaining social cohesion, than in situations of inequality. In this light, Mauss's priorities for the good society do not turn out be incompatible. Individuality and the obligation to work and defend one's own interests (from self to society) do not exclude society's obligations to return the gift (through education, income protection, fair prices for food and housing, fair wages for services, and protection of health and life). The key is a more comprehensive view of individualism, as Mauss's recommended steps against greed, accumulation, and unrestricted profit-taking demand changes to a legal framework that is based on a utilitarian vision of the individual. Current scholarship on the relationship between high levels of social integration and more favorable economic, health, education, and crime statistics lends further support to Mauss's vision in *The Gift*.[10]

1. Marcel Mauss, *The Gift: The Form and Reason for Exchange in Archaic Societies* (London: Routledge, 1990), 5–6.

2. Marilyn Strathern, *The Gender of the Gift: Problems with Women and Problems with Society in Melanesia* (Berkeley: University of California Press, 1988); Annette Weiner, *Women of Value, Men of Renown: New Perspectives in Trobriand Exchange* (Austin: University of Texas Press, 1976).

3. Mauss mentions the "Pygmies" of Central Africa. They lived in forests near villagers and were known to missionaries and other foreigners long before most other groups of foragers.

4. Marshall Sahlins, *Stone Age Economics* (New York: Aldine de Gruyter, 1972), 1.

5. Marshall Sahlins, *The Western Illusion of Human Nature: With Reflections on the Long History of Hierarchy, Equality and the Sublimation of Anarchy in the West, and Comparative Notes on Other Conceptions of the Human Condition* (Chicago: Prickly Paradigm Press, 2008).

6. Douglas P. Fry, *The Human Potential for Peace: An Anthropological Challenge to Assumptions about War and Violence* (New York: Oxford University Press, 2006).

7. Fry, *The Human Potential*.

8. Lee Cronk, "Strings Attached," *The Sciences* 29, no. 3 (1988): 2–4.

9. Ernestine Friedl, "Society and Sex Roles," *Human Nature* 1 (1978): 8–75.

10. Marcel Mauss, *The Gift*, 68–89; Richard Wilkinson and Kate Pickett, *The Spirit Level: Why Greater Equality Makes Societies Stronger* (New York: Bloomsbury Press, 2009).

MODULE 12
WHERE NEXT?

KEY POINTS

* *The Gift* is a seminal text for its contributions to knowledge about the connection between gift cycles and social relationships, its participation in a trajectory of ideas, and its capacity to launch new ideas as times change.
* Mauss's work on the sacred* or magical elements of reciprocal* gift exchange is likely to extend the book's impact further into the future.
* Mauss's analysis of giving and receiving, including the transfer of mystical qualities, is relevant to scholarship on the trade in body organs and tissues, social relationships in the age of social media, and other concerns of current times.

Potential

The sacred elements of gift exchange explored by Marcel Mauss in *The Gift* point to many possibilities for further investigation. To illustrate, Mauss notes that in archaic societies* religious sacrifice is a means for people to maintain reciprocal obligations with the divine.[1] This involves gifts to the spirits as well as alms to the poor, in recognition of past favor and as an instrument through which to draw continued benefits. Research on the degree to which religious feeling motivates charitable giving in commercial societies is one avenue for Mauss's influence to be felt. His proposal that the rich be encouraged to see themselves as the temporary custodians of wealth obtained through some kind of supernatural favor, with corresponding duties as the financial guardians of others, has a place in contemporary debates about tax laws, charitable giving, and education and social services. These would need to address the contradiction, pointed out by Mauss, between giving as a spiritual obligation and the fact that sacred gift cycles support the social system as it stands.

Another path for Mauss's ideas is the role of magic in modern society. It has been pointed out that people in Western society continue to attribute supernatural power to things like special foods favored by ancient peoples, or spring water drawn from faraway places.[2] Popular concepts such as *karma* (the Buddhist and Hindu belief that accumulated merit determines one's fortune in this or subsequent lives) and "paying it forward" (performing positive actions as part of a cycle of good) suggest a perception that supernatural forces are at work in individual lives, that people are interconnected in mysterious ways, and that there can be distant consequences to one's daily actions. This is in spite of a return to utilitarianism* in economics and politics (a return to highly pragmatic assumptions and policies in which utility is favored over considerations that cannot be measured, such as ethics), and the veneration of science. The sacred or magical meaning alive in contemporary culture provides an enormous field for analysis inspired by Mauss's ideas.

> *"Human organs are regularly subjected to elaborate metaphorical reworking that ultimately silences [ethical] unease. The most pervasive and obvious example involves relabeling organs as 'gifts of life,' a process that quickly mystifies the economic realities of their origins."*
>
> ——Lesley Sharp,* "Commodified Kin: Death, Mourning, and Competing Claims on the Bodies of Organ Donors in the United States"

Future Directions

Mauss's book suggests that a pure gift given out of generosity and without any expectation of a return is a logical impossibility, for there is always the potential for hidden nonmaterial benefits such as prestige or self-gratification. In relation to blood donation, Richard Titmuss,* the British founder of the academic discipline of social policy, allows that donors may experience social approval and feel that they might some day need a transfusion themselves, but argues that they consciously give blood as a moral act for the sake of social solidarity.*3 To encourage donations, then, the gift must be isolated from the corrupting influence of money.

The medical anthropologist Margaret Lock* argues, however, that this separation derives from an artificial and unnecessarily stark distinction between market* and reciprocal exchange. She notes that when traditional economies become integrated into the market, they do not shed existing systems of reciprocal gift exchange but rather maintain a set of parallel or hybrid institutions.*4 Likewise, in the donation industry, a framework for biological transfers based on transactions coexists with an unrecognized system of reciprocal exchange in which gifts carry social obligations.

Lock explains that the transplant industry purposely "fetishizes" organs in the sense used by the influential German economist and political philosopher Karl Marx: * they become objects of extraordinary value in a process Marx termed "commodity objectification," obscuring the exploitative relationships in production and consumption. Lock argues that organs are also fetishized in the original sense, recognized by Mauss, of being endowed with individuality and magical power:"Body parts remain infused with life and even personality ... Once an organ is procured and transferred, the recipient is severely reprimanded, even thought of as exhibiting pathology, if he attributes this life-saving organ with animistic* qualities."[5]

Medical staff take pains to define the gift as freely given, skirting ethical questions through the concept of the gift-as-object detached from all suffering as well as corporate interest. The system presents organs as literally disembodied commodities (roughly, useful objects) with no human content and no capacity to generate obligations—but donor and recipient families know otherwise and build relationships just the same.[6]

Summary

Mauss shows that gifts bind individuals, families, societies, and nations in a perpetual cycle of mutual indebtedness. Gifts are alive with personhood* and spiritual values. They demand to be repaid, one way or another. These ideas are highly relevant to contemporary society, useful for analyzing the economic and moral dimensions of voluntary biological transfers including, increasingly, DNA—the biological material in which genetic information is encoded and passed down.[7] Mauss's insights shed light on voluntary gifts of money for business development or personal needs through crowdfunding (the practice of raising money for small ventures through personal donations, especially via online communities), and knowledge through open source software, free content, and websites that serve as nodes for technical and creative exchanges.[8]

In addition, Mauss's analysis suggests how purely commercial transactions represent missed opportunities for building social solidarity. Gift cycles dictate a time lag that projects the relationship into the future; although this may be against the people's will, it brings them concrete benefits. Research has confirmed that greater social cohesiveness improves health and mental well-being, and that the extent of mutual obligations is connected to the degree of social solidarity. Mauss's desire to work out how individual autonomy can be reconciled with social embeddedness in mass society—that is, the ways in which economic behavior is constrained by society's non-economic institutions—has been fulfilled by studies on clubs and volunteer associations. In these subgroups of large industrialized societies, social cohesiveness arises out of mutual obligations and the active avoidance of hierarchy, and is favorable to individual well-being.[9]

Mauss has taught generations of readers that gifts are both expressive and instrumental. Exchanges between people—as individuals or as members of a group—take part within larger systems of rules, inequalities, and power. Whether they involve money, material goods, or purely intangible things, transfers carry culturally constructed symbolic values and meanings and strengthen social relationships.

1. H. Hubert and M. Mauss, *Sacrifice: Its Nature and Functions* (London: Routledge, 1964).

2. Marshall Sahlins, *The Western Illusion of Human Nature: With Reflections on the Long History of Hierarchy, Equality and the Sublimation of Anarchy in the West, and Comparative Notes on Other Conceptions of the Human Condition* (Chicago: Prickly Paradigm Press, 2008).

3. Richard Titmuss, *The Gift Relationship: From Human Blood to Social Policy* (New York: New Press, 1997).

4. Margaret Lock, *Twice Dead: Organ Transplants and the Reinvention of Death* (Berkeley: University of California Press, 2001), 316.

5. Lock, *Twice Dead*, 320.

6. Lesley A. Sharp, "Commodified Kin: Death, Mourning, and Competing Claims on the Bodies of Organ Donors in the United States," *American Anthropologist* 103, no. 1 (2001): 112–33.

7. Deepa Reddy, "Good Gifts for a Common Good: Blood and Bioethics in the Market of Genetic Research," *Cultural Anthropology* 22, no. 3 (2007): 429–72.

8. Christopher Kelty, *Two Bits: The Cultural Significance of Free Software* (Durham, NC: Duke University Press, 2008).

9. Richard Wilkinson and Kate Pickett, *The Spirit Level: Why Greater Equality Makes Societies Stronger* (New York: Bloomsbury Press, 2009).

GLOSSARY OF TERMS

1. **Affinity:** the principle of "like attracts like" and the basis for "sympathetic magic," by which rituals such as rain dances imitate the thing desired.

2. **Agency:** the freedom and resources necessary for knowing and realizing one's own will.

3. **Ancient Eurasia:** ancient civilizations including Greek, Roman, Indian, and Middle Eastern societies.

4. **Animism:** a belief in spirits.

5. *L'Année Sociologique*: a journal established in 1898 by French social scientist Émile Durkheim to publish his own work and that of his students in the new discipline of sociology, which he had founded.

6. **Anthropology:** the study of the biological and cultural history and current variability of humankind.

7. **Anti-Semitism:** animosity, prejudice, and discrimination directed at Jews or Judaism.

8. **Archaic societies:** Mauss's term for contemporary indigenous societies as well as ancient civilizations representing a middle stage of social evolution.

9. **Barter:** the exchange of dissimilar items on the spot and possibly involving bargaining.

10. **Bolshevism:** the movement by which the Russian Social Democratic Workers' Party worked from 1903 to 1917 to seize power, establish a communist government, and within five years create the Union of Soviet Socialist Republics.

11. **Capitalism:** the economic and social model founded on the private ownership of industry and business that is dominant in the West (and increasingly throughout the Western world) today.

12. **Clan:** a group of relatives (whether by blood or marriage) whose kinship is based on the belief that they share a common ancestor.

13. **Collective representations:** shared beliefs and understandings.

14. **Collectivism:** ethical, political, and social philosophies focused on the group and opposed to individualism.

15. **Comparative analysis:** a comparison of societies or groups through their

different social systems, artifacts, or features.

16. **Contagion:** the principle in "primitive" magic derived from belief in the permanent presence of mystical forces in things such as body products, which allows for manipulation of these forces through contact with the infused object.

17. **Cooperative movement:** a nineteenth-century European promotion of alternative economic institutions in response to social upheaval and labor insecurity associated with the Industrial Revolution and the mechanization of production.

18. **Culture:** a dynamic and unbounded set of beliefs, behavioral expectations, values, creative forms, and knowledge shared by a group of people.

19. **Currency:** any medium of exchange, from shells and agricultural products to gold and paper money.

20. **Empirical approach:** the idea that all knowledge should be gained by experience, by using experiments and observation to gather facts.

21. **Eskimo:** indigenous peoples of the Far North, including the Arctic coasts of North America, Greenland, and Siberia; also known as Inuit.

22. **Ethnography:** the systematic study of a group of people through long-term immersion and knowledge of the local language; also used to refer to a written analysis of data gathered through fieldwork.

23. **Ethnology:** the discipline concerned with analysis of ethnographic data and cross-cultural similarities and differences.

24. **Foraging:** a way of life based on food collection rather than cultivation or herding; also known as hunting and gathering.

25. **French Workers' Party:** a socialist political party in France formed in 1880 and merged into the French Socialist Party in 1905.

26. **Habitus:** in antiquity, the combination of constitutional and environmental forces that shapes individual physical existence and specific vulnerabilities to disease. In current academic usage, the concept emphasizes the embodiment of social and cultural conditions.

27. *Hau:* the Maori concept for the power of a certain class of gifts that compels people to pass them on and allow them to return to their place of origin.

28. **Historical particularism:** a theoretical movement in anthropology associated with Franz Boas that stresses the importance of recording details of group life in relation to historical context and attending to the uniqueness of individual societies.

29. **Holistic:** concerned with the whole and the interdependence of parts.

30. **Indigenous peoples:** the original inhabitants of a territory; often used in reference to people displaced or marginalized by governments or settlers from elsewhere.

31. **Institut d'Ethnologie:** the French ethnological institute founded in 1925 by Lucien Lévy-Bruhl, Marcel Mauss, and Paul Rivet.

32. **Institution:** a conventional relationship or activity such as marriage or retirement; also, a formal, legal entity such as a school or court of law.

33. **Kinship:** the bond between people that arises through birth, marriage, baptism, adoption, and other social means of defining relatedness.

34. *Kula:* a circular ceremonial exchange of armbands and necklaces in opposite directions from one island to another in the Trobriand Islands.

35. **Liberalism:** a political philosophy based on autonomous individualism, free market economics, and law-based governance free of interference in individual liberties.

36. *Mana:* the Polynesian and Melanesian concept of a pervasive spiritual force that permeates the universe, can attach to objects, and reveals itself through some people's advantages and powers.

37. **Maori:** the indigenous people of New Zealand.

38. **Market economy:** the economic exchange of goods based on established calculated values, not limited to exchange in actual physical markets.

39. **Melanesia:** the group of islands in the southwestern Pacific Ocean between the equator and northeast Australia, including the Solomon Islands, New Caledonia, and Papua New Guinea.

40. **Personhood:** the state of being an individual within a particular cultural and social context. In Western thought a "person" is a social individual while "selfhood" refers to the individual's internal experience.

41. **Polynesia:** the scattered islands in the south-central Pacific Ocean situated between New Zealand, Hawaii, and Easter Island.

42. **Poststructuralism:** A variety of theoretical and methodological approaches that reject the principle of binary oppositions central to structuralism and emphasize fluidity and change in conceptual categories and their meanings.

43. *Potlatch:* a ceremonial feast practiced by Native American populations in Northwest North America that includes gifts to the guests; between rival groups, a means for the competitive display of wealth and prestige through quantitatively increasing gifts and even the destruction of wealth objects.

44. **Pygmies:** indigenous peoples of the Central African forests.

45. **Rationality:** in economics, a characteristic of reasoning through which marginal costs and benefits are weighed in order to maximize utility.

46. **Reciprocity:** the cyclic exchange of material and intangible gifts and services between individuals or groups.

47. **Revolutionary Socialist Workers' Party:** a moderate reformers' party in France from 1890 to 1901 that promoted education and labor safeguards.

48. **Sacred:** a category and adjective referring to the sphere of ideas, rituals, and objects worthy of religious veneration.

49. **Seasonality:** changes in people's patterns of behavior according to the season of the year.

50. **Social evolutionism:** the belief that societies progress through a fixed series of stages of ever-increasing technological, social, and intellectual perfection; and that differences in the speed of evolution account for the coexistence of variably advanced societies.

51. **Socialism:** a political system in which the means of production (the tools and resources required by business and industry) are held in common ownership.

52. **Sociology:** the study of social behavior, social institutions, and the origins and organization of human society.

53. **Solidarity:** the degree of connectedness people feel for one another.

54. **Soviet Union:** the Union of Soviet Socialist Republics (USSR), a large Eurasian

country that arose from the Russian Revolution in 1917 and consisted of Russia and 14 satellite states in Eastern Europe, the Baltic and Black Seas, and Central Asia, existing from 1922 to 1991.

55. **Structural-functionalism:** a theoretical approach in anthropology and sociology associated with A. R. Radcliffe-Brown and Bronislaw Malinowski that focuses on the ways in which societies are structured and the internal parts are integrated with one another.

56. **Structuralism:** an approach to the analysis of social, textual, or linguistic forms that involves arranging elemental components into a system of binary opposition; associated in anthropology with Claude Lévi-Strauss.

57. **Totem:** a neutral object that is infused with sacredness; the object through which a group of people symbolizes itself.

58. **Trade:** the formalized exchange of unalike items according to prescribed standards of value.

59. **Tribes:** a category of societies that are politically organized around kinship relations.

60. **Utilitarianism:** the idea that usefulness determines the value of things; eighteenth- and nineteenth-century English philosophical tradition associated with Jeremy Bentham and John Stuart Mill based on the ethical goal of maximizing utility for the collective, defined as the surfeit of well-being that remains after correcting for suffering (concisely, the greatest good for the greatest number of people).

61. **Utility:** in economics, the material and/or psychological usefulness to an individual consumer of purchased goods and services.

62. **World War I:** the war fought between 1914 and 1918 in which Austria-Hungary, Germany, Turkey, and Bulgaria were defeated by Great Britain, France, Italy, Russia, Japan, the United States, and other allies.

63. **World War II:** a global conflict from 1939 to 1945 that involved the world's great powers and numerous other countries around the globe. Fought between the Allies (the United States, Britain, France, the Soviet Union, and others) and the Axis powers (Germany, Italy, Japan, and others), it was seen as a major moral struggle between freedom and tyranny.

1. **Fredrik Barth (b. 1928)** is a Norwegian anthropologist with a wide range of fieldwork experience. He is known for works on political and economic organization, ethnicity, and knowledge.

2. **Georges Bataille (1897–1962)** was a French writer and philosopher whose work spanned the humanistic disciplines and included transgressive novels and short stories.

3. **Henri Beauchat (1878–1914)** was a French sociologist and colleague of Durkheim and Mauss. He died of exposure and starvation on an island off the northeastern coast of Siberia along with other members of an expedition.

4. **Ruth Benedict (1887–1948)** was an American anthropologist interested in folklore, art, language, and personality. She is known for her comparative study of cultures and insights into the performative aspects of culture.

5. **Jeremy Bentham (1748–1832)** was a British jurist and philosopher, and founder of philosophical utilitarianism.

6. **Helmuth Berking (b. 1952)** is a German sociologist interested in economic and urban anthropology, social theory, and cultural identity.

7. **Gérald Berthoud (b. 1935)** is a Swiss sociologist and economist and cofounder with Alain Caillé of the Anti-Utilitarian Movement in the Social Sciences.

8. **Maurice Bloch (b. 1939)** is a British anthropologist who has carried out fieldwork in Madagascar. He is a distinguished academic and was a professor at the London School of Economics from 1983 onward.

9. **Franz Boas (1858–1942)** was a German American anthropologist associated with historical particularism in American anthropology and the study of Native Americans of the Northwest Coast. He is considered the "father of American anthropology."

10. **Pierre Bourdieu (1930–2002)** was a French sociologist, philosopher, and anthropologist interested in reflexivity, language, and the social sources and dynamics of power. He is known for concepts such as habitus and social, symbolic, and cultural capital.

11. **Alain Caillé (b. 1944)** is a French sociologist and economist, cofounder of the

Anti-Utilitarian Movement in the Social Sciences, editor of the journal *MAUSS*, and author of numerous books inspired by *The Gift*.

12. **Roger Caillois (1913–78)** was a French writer, sociologist, and political philosopher. He is known for his work on the sacred, games and play, and Latin American literature.

13. **Georges Condominas (1921–2011)** was a French anthropologist who conducted research in Vietnam and was taught by Denise Paulme, Marcel Griaule, and Maurice Leenhardt.

14. **Charles Darwin (1809–82)** was a British naturalist, most famous for his work on evolutionary theory, and specifically for developing the theory of natural selection, the belief that all animals are descended from a common ancestor.

15. **Jacques Derrida (1930–2004)** was a French sociologist born in Algeria who pioneered a strain of symbolic analysis known as deconstruction.

16. **Georges Devereux (1908–85)** was a Hungarian French anthropologist and psychoanalyst, and close associate of Claude Lévi-Strauss. He is considered the father of ethnopsychiatry.

17. **Mary Douglas (1921–2007)** was a British social anthropologist interested in symbolism, comparative religion, and economic and environmental anthropology. She is best known for her structuralist analysis of sacred categories, *Purity and Danger* (1966).

18. **Alfred Dreyfus (1859–1935)** was a French artillery officer of Jewish background who in 1895 was sentenced by secret court martial to life imprisonment in exile for treason. A scandal over the "Dreyfus Affair" led to his receiving a presidential pardon in 1899. In 1906, Dreyfus was officially exonerated by the military and returned to service.

19. **Émile Durkheim (1858–1917)** was a French social scientist considered the founder of sociology. Durkheim's sociology fuses Comte's positivist sociology with a humanistic focus on shared beliefs and values. He is best known for his writings on alienation, suicide, and sociological methods.

20. **Alfred Victor Espinas (1844–1922)** was a French philosopher who wrote

about political philosophy, intellectual history, and the evolution of human thought.

21. **Edward Evan Evans-Pritchard (1902–73)** was one of the founders of British social anthropology and a follower of Radcliffe-Brown's structural-functionalism. He is known for studies on the Azande and Nuer in South Sudan.

22. **Paul Fauconnet (1874–1938)** was a French sociologist and member of the original group formed around the journal *L'Année Sociologique*.

23. **Raymond Firth (1901–2002)** was an anthropologist from New Zealand who taught for many decades at the London School of Economics and disputed Marcel Mauss's interpretation of certain Maori beliefs discussed in *The Gift*.

24. **James George Frazer (1854–1941)** was a Scottish sociologist and anthropologist who compiled 12 volumes of religious beliefs from around the world, organized according to his belief that human thought progressed from magic to religion to science. *The Golden Bough* was published in three editions in 1890, 1900, and 1906–15.

25. **Ernestine Friedl (b. 1920)** is a Hungarian-born American anthropologist with interests in gender, rural Greece, and the Chippewa of Wisconsin. She is known for a seminal article on "Society and Sex Roles."

26. **Clifford Geertz (1926–2006)** was an American anthropologist who conducted fieldwork in Indonesia. Together with Victor Turner, he is considered the founder of symbolic and interpretive anthropology.

27. **Maurice Godelier (b. 1934)** is a French philosopher and anthropologist who conducted fieldwork in Papua New Guinea. He is known for his contributions to economic and development anthropology and the analysis of inequality, gender, and power.

28. **Walter Goldschmidt (1903–2010)** was an American anthropologist with a wide range of fieldwork experience and interests. He is known for his analysis of the implications of industrial versus small, independent farming for local communities in California.

29. **Octave Hamelin (1856–1907)** was a French philosopher at the University of

Bordeaux who was a close associate of Durkheim's.

30. **Robert Hertz (1881–1915)** was a French sociologist of religion and close colleague of Durkheim and Mauss. He was killed in World War I.

31. **Henri Hubert (1872–1927)** was a French historian and sociologist interested in religion who collaborated closely with Mauss on essays and book reviews.

32. **Lewis Hyde (b. 1945)** is an American writer, critic, and translator. He is known for his work on creativity and commerce.

33. **Richard Hyland (b. 1949)** is an American writer and legal scholar. He is known for his comparative and historical analysis of informal and formal laws concerning gift-giving.

34. **Jacques Lacan (1901–81)** was a French psychoanalyst and scholar of sociology, literary theory, and linguistics. He was the intellectual center of poststructuralism.

35. **Maurice Leenhardt (1878–1954)** was a French clergyman and anthropologist who conducted fieldwork in New Caledonia. He was a follower of Mauss's teachings on methodology, and is considered the founder of Melanesian anthropology.

36. **Claude Lévi-Strauss (1908–2009)** was a French sociologist born in Belgium and the "father of structuralism."

37. **Henri Lévy-Bruhl (1884–1964)** was a French sociologist trained by Mauss who was interested in comparative law, religion, and modes of thought.

38. **Lucien Lévy-Bruhl (1857–1939)** was a French philosopher and sociologist interested in the evolution of the mind. Together with Mauss and Paul Rivet, he helped found the Institut d'Ethnologie in Paris.

39. **Harry Liebersohn (b. 1951)** is an American historian who is interested in intellectual history, social theory, travel writing, religion, creativity, and gift exchange.

40. **Margaret Lock (b. 1936)** is a British-born Canadian anthropologist specializing in medical anthropology. She is known for her work on aging, organ transplants, and comparative medical knowledge and practices.

41. **Bronislaw Malinowski (1884–1942)** was a Polish anthropologist, sociologist, and ethnographer who is considered the cofounder (with A. R. Radcliffe-Brown) of British social anthropology. He is best known for his work on the *kula* gift exchange system in the Trobriand Islands.

42. **Jean-Luc Marion (b. 1946)** is a French philosopher known for his work on religion, love, and giving.

43. **Karl Marx (1818–83)** was a highly influential economist and social theorist; Marxist theory, a method of social and historical analysis that emphasizes the struggle between the classes, among other things, is derived from his works, notably *Capital* (1867–94) and *The Communist Manifesto* (1848).

44. **Margaret Mead (1901–78)** was an American anthropologist and public figure who conducted research in Melanesia and the South Pacific on gender roles, sexuality, childrearing, and adolescence.

45. **John Stuart Mill (1806–73)** was a British civil servant and political and economic philosopher who believed that individual economic initiative and responsibility were the basis of liberty.

46. **Lewis Henry Morgan (1818–81)** was an American lawyer, politician, and anthropologist who studied kinship, social structure, and customs according to the belief that societies progressed from savagery to barbarism to civilization.

47. **Denise Paulme (1909–98)** was one of the first academically trained female French anthropologists. She was one of Mauss's students and studied literature, ritual, and social and political organization in African societies beginning in the 1930s.

48. **Karl Polanyi (1886–1964)** was a Hungarian American philosopher, anthropologist, social historian, and political-economist. He was the originator of the sociocultural approach to economics known as substantivism and is best known for his 1944 book, *The Great Transformation*.

49. **Alfred Reginald Radcliffe-Brown (1881–1955)** was a British philosopher, psychologist, and anthropologist known as the "father of British structural-functionalism."Together with Bronislaw Malinowski, he is considered the

founder of British social anthropology.

50. **Paul Ricoeur (1913–2005)** was a French philosopher interested in history, psychology, identity, language, literary criticism, and theological studies. His work on Christian theology was influenced by Mauss's analysis of reciprocal exchange.

51. **Paul Rivet (1876–1958)** was a French physician and ethnographer who conducted research in South America. Together with Mauss and Lucien Lévy-Bruhl, he helped found the Institut d'Ethnologie in Paris.

52. **Jean Rouch (1917–2004)** was a French anthropologist and filmmaker who worked for decades in Africa and is known for his technique of blending documentary and fictional elements in film.

53. **Marshall Sahlins (b. 1930)** is an American anthropologist who conducted fieldwork in the Pacific and has made significant contributions to anthropological theory. He is a professor emeritus of anthropology and social sciences at the University of Chicago.

54. **Ferdinand de Saussure (1857–1913)** was a Swiss linguist who is considered a founding father of modern linguistics and the study of meaning-making or signification. He is best known for his posthumously published lectures on linguistics.

55. **Alan Schrift (b. 1955)** is an American philosopher who is interested in nineteenth- and twentieth-century philosophy and the theme of generosity and giving.

56. **Lesley Sharp (b. 1956)** is an American medical anthropologist who has done fieldwork in Madagascar. She is known for her work on body commodification and the social construction of the self.

57. **Georg Simmel (1858–1918)** was a German philosopher and sociologist, and author of a seminal work on economic systems as social and cultural systems, *The Philosophy of Money*.

58. **Herbert Spencer (1820–1903)** was a British philosopher who advanced a comprehensive evolutionary theory by which species, nature, society, and the

human mind progressed from simple to complex forms.

59. **Marilyn Strathern (b. 1941)** is a British anthropologist who has conducted fieldwork in Papua New Guinea. She is known for her work on gender, kinship, and reproduction, which has challenged earlier anthropologists' interpretations of exchange in Melanesia.

60. **Richard Titmuss (1907–73)** was a self-taught British scholar who founded the academic discipline of social policy in England. He is known for his work on giving and altruism in relation to social and health policy.

61. **Alexis de Tocqueville (1805–59)** was a French historian and political theorist. He is best known for his analysis of political economy and social conditions in the United States, *Democracy in America* (1835 and 1840).

62. **Victor Turner (1920–83)** was a Scottish social anthropologist known for his work in Africa on rites of passage, ritual, and symbols. Together with Clifford Geertz, he is considered the founder of symbolic and interpretive anthropology.

63. **Edward Burnett Tylor (1832–1917)** was a British anthropologist who advanced a social evolutionary approach to the study of cultures. He is considered one of the founders of academic anthropology.

64. **Thorstein Veblen (1857–1929)** was an American sociologist and economist who developed the concept of conspicuous consumption to describe competitive spending behavior. He wrote *The Theory of the Leisure Class* (1899).

65. **Max Weber (1864–1920)** was a German scholar with Marcel Mauss's same interests and expertise in law, philosophy, economics, and sociology. He is best known for *The Protestant Ethic and the Spirit of Capitalism*.

66. **Annette Weiner (1933–97)** was an American anthropologist who conducted fieldwork in the Trobriand Islands a half-century after Malinowski. She is known for her work on the social and political roles of women in relation to reciprocal exchange systems.

67. **Émile Zola (1840–1902)** was a French novelist and playwright who promoted naturalism in fiction. He is known for his 1898 letter, "J'Accuse," in defense of the falsely accused French army officer Alfred Dreyfus.

WORKS CITED

1. Barth, Fredrik, Robert Parkin, Andre Gingrich, and Sydel Silverman. *One Discipline, Four Ways: British, German, French, and American Anthropology.* Chicago: University of Chicago Press, 2005.

2. Benedict, Ruth. *Patterns of Culture.* New York: Houghton Mifflin, 2005.

3. Berking, Helmuth. *Sociology of Giving: Theory, Culture, and Society.* Translated by Patrick Camiller. London: Sage Publications, 1999.

4. Boas, Franz. "The Limitations of the Comparative Method of Anthropology." *Science* 4, no. 103 (1896): 901–8.

5. "Changes in Bodily Form of Descendants of Immigrants." *American Anthropologist* 14, no. 3 (1912): 530–62.

6. *Race, Language, and Culture.* London: Collier-Macmillan, 1940.

7. *Kwakiutl Ethnography.* Chicago: University of Chicago Press, 1966.

8. Bohannan, Paul, and Mark Glazer (eds). *High Points in Anthropology.* New York: Alfred A. Knopf, 1988.

9. Bourdieu, Pierre. *Outline of a Theory of Practice.* Cambridge: Cambridge University Press, 1977.

10. Caillé, Alain. *Anthropologie du Don: Le Tiers Paradigme.* Paris: Desclée de Brouwer, 2000.

11. Condominas, Georges. "Marcel Mauss, Père de l'ethnographie française." *Critique* 28, no. 297 (1972): 118–39.

12. Cronk, Lee. "Strings Attached." *The Sciences* 29, no. 3 (1988): 2–4.

13. Derrida, Jacques. *Given Time.* Chicago: University of Chicago Press, 1992.

14. *The Gift of Death.* Chicago: University of Chicago Press, 2007.

15. Dobrin, Lise M., and Ira Bashkow. "'Arapesh Warfare': Reo Fortune's Veiled Critique of Margaret Mead's *Sex and Temperament.*" *American Anthropologist* 112, no. 3 (2010): 370–83.

16. Douglas, Mary. "Foreword: No Free Gifts." In *The Gift,* by Marcel Mauss. London: Routledge, 2000.

17. Durkheim, Émile. *The Elementary Forms of the Religious Life.* New York: Free

Press, 1915.

18. *The Division of Labor in Society.* New York: Free Press, 1984.

19. *On Suicide.* London: Penguin Books, 2006.

20. Durkheim, Émile, and Marcel Mauss. *Primitive Classification.* Chicago: University of Chicago Press, 1963.

21. Evans-Pritchard, E. E. *The Nuer: A Description of the Modes of Livelihood and Political Institutions of a Nilotic People.* Oxford: Clarendon Press, 1940.

22. Fauconnet, Paul, and Marcel Mauss. "Sociologie: Objet et Méthode." *La Grande Encyclopédie* 30 (1901): 165–76.

23. Firth, Raymond. *Primitive Economics of the New Zealand Maori.* London: Routledge, 1929.

24. Fournier, Marcel. *Marcel Mauss: A Biography.* Princeton, NJ: Princeton University Press, 2005.

25. Frazer, James George. *The Illustrated Golden Bough: A Study in Magic and Religion.* New York: Simon and Schuster, 1996.

26. Friedl, Ernestine. "Society and Sex Roles." *Human Nature* 1 (1978): 8–75.

27. Fry, Douglas P. *The Human Potential for Peace: An Anthropological Challenge to Assumptions about War and Violence.* New York: Oxford University Press, 2006.

28. Geertz, Clifford. "From the Native's Point of View." In *Local Knowledge,* by Clifford Geertz, 54–70. New York: Basic Books, 1983.

29. Godbout, Jacques, and Alain Caillé. *L'Esprit du Don.* Montréal and Paris: Éditions La Découverte, 1992.

30. Godelier, Maurice. *L'Enigme du Don.* Paris: Fayard, 1996.

31. Goldschmidt, Walter. "Untitled Review of *The Gift* by Marcel Mauss." *American Anthropologist* 57, no. 6 (1955): 1299–1300.

32. Hubert, Henri, and Marcel Mauss. *Sacrifice: its Nature and Functions.* Routledge: London, 1964.

33. Hyde, Lewis. *The Gift: Imagination and the Erotic Life of Property.* New York: Vintage Books, 2008.

34. Hyland, Richard. *Gifts: A Study in Comparative Law.* Oxford: Oxford University

Press, 2009.

35. Kelty, Christopher. *Two Bits: The Cultural Significance of Free Software.* Durham, NC: Duke University Press, 2008.

36. Leacock, Seth. "The Ethnological Theory of Marcel Mauss." *American Anthropologist* 56 (1954): 58–71.

37. Lévi-Strauss, Claude. *The Elementary Structures of Kinship.* Boston: Beacon Press, 1969.

38. *Introduction to the Work of Marcel Mauss.* London: Routledge and Kegan Paul, 1987.

39. Liebersohn, Harry. *The Return of the Gift: European History of a Global Idea.* New York: Cambridge University Press, 2011.

40. Lock, Margaret. *Twice Dead: Organ Transplants and the Reinvention of Death.* Berkeley: University of California Press, 2001.

41. Malinowski, Bronislaw. *Argonauts of the Western Pacific: An Account of Native Enterprise and Adventure in the Archipelagos of Melanesian New Guinea.* London: Routledge, 1922.

42. Marion, Jean-Luc. *Being Given: Toward a Phenomenology of Givenness.* Palo Alta, CA: Stanford University Press, 2002.

43. Mauss, Marcel. "L'Enseignement de l'Histoire des Religions des Peuples Non-Civilisés à l'École des Hautes Études." *Revue de l'Histoire des Religions* 45 (1902): 36–55.

44. "Essai sur le Don: Forme et Raison de l'Échange dans les Sociétés Archaïques." *Année Sociologique* no. 1 (1923–4): 30–186.

45. "Effet Physique chez l'Individu de l'Idée de Mort Suggérée par la Collectivité." *Journal de Psychologie Normale et Pathologique* XXIII, no. 6 (1926): 653–69.

46. "Les Techniques du Corps." *Journal de Psychologie Normale et Pathologique* XXXII, nos 3–4 (1934): 271–93.

47. "Une Catégorie de l'Esprit Humain: La Notion de Personne, celle de 'Moi.'" *Journal of the Royal Anthropological Institute* XLVIII, no. 2 (1938): 263–81.

48. *Manuel d'Ethnographie.* Paris: Payot, 1947.

49. *Sociologie et Anthropologie.* Paris: Presses Universaires de France, 1950.

50. *The Gift: Forms and Functions of Exchange in Archaic Societies*. Glencoe, IL: Free Press, 1954.

51. "L'Oeuvre de Mauss par Lui-Même." *Revue Française de Sociologie* 20, nos 20–1 (1979).

52. *The Gift: The Form and Reason for Exchange in Archaic Societies*. London: Routledge, 1990.

53. *The Gift: Expanded Edition*. Chicago: University of Chicago Press for HAU, 2015.

54. Mauss, Marcel, and Henri Beauchat. *Seasonal Variation of the Eskimo: A Study in Social Morphology*. London: Routledge, 1979 (1906).

55. Mauss, Marcel, and Henri Hubert. "Essai sur la Nature et la Fonction du Sacrifice." *L'Année Sociologique* (1897–8): 29–138.

56. *A General Theory of Magic*. London: Routledge, 2001.

57. Mead, Margaret. *Sex and Temperament in Three Primitive Societies*. New York: William Morrow, 1935.

58. Morgan, Lewis Henry. *Ancient Society: Researches into the Lines of Human Progress from Savagery through Barbarism to Civilization*. New York: Henry Holt and Company, 1877.

59. Polanyi, Karl. *The Great Transformation: The Political and Economic Origins of Our Time*. New York: Farrar and Rinehart, 1944.

60. Radcliffe-Brown, Alfred Reginald. "Three Tribes of Western Australia." *Journal of the Royal Anthropological Institute* XLIII (1913).

61. *The Andaman Islanders*. Cambridge: Cambridge University Press, 1933.

62. Reddy, Deepa. "Good Gifts for a Common Good: Blood and Bioethics in the Market of Genetic Research." *Cultural Anthropology* 22, no. 3 (2007): 429–72.

63. Ricoeur, Paul. *History, Memory, Forgetting*. Chicago: University of Chicago Press, 2004.

64. Sahlins, Marshall. *Stone Age Economics*. New York: Aldine de Gruyter, 1972.

65. *Apologies to Thucydides: Understanding History as Culture and Vice Versa*. Chicago: University of Chicago Press, 2004.

66. *The Western Illusion of Human Nature: With Reflections on the Long History*

of Hierarchy, Equality and the Sublimation of Anarchy in the West, and Comparative Notes on Other Conceptions of the Human Condition. Chicago: Prickly Paradigm Press, 2008.

67. De Saussure, Ferdinand. *Course in General Linguistics*. Translated by Wade Baskin. New York: McGraw-Hill, 1959.

68. Schrift, Alan D. (ed.). *The Logic of the Gift: Toward an Ethic of Generosity*. London: Routledge, 1997.

69. Sharp, Lesley A. "Commodified Kin: Death, Mourning, and Competing Claims on the Bodies of Organ Donors in the United States." *American Anthropologist* 103, no. 1 (2001): 112–33.

70. Simmel, Georg. *The Philosophy of Money*. London: Routledge, 1978.

71. Strathern, Marilyn. *The Gender of the Gift: Problems with Women and Problems with Society in Melanesia*. Berkeley: University of California Press, 1988.

72. Titmuss, Richard. *The Gift Relationship: From Human Blood to Social Policy*. New York: New Press, 1997.

73. Turner, Victor. *The Ritual Process: Structure and Anti-Structure*. Chicago: Aldine, 1969.

74. *Dramas, Fields, and Metaphors: Symbolic Action in Human Society*. Ithaca, NY: Cornell University Press, 1974.

75. Tylor, Edward Burnett. *Primitive Culture: Researches into the Development of Mythology, Philosophy, Religion, Art, and Custom*. London: J. Murray, 1871.

76. Veblen, Thorstein. *The Theory of the Leisure Class: An Economic Study of the Evolution of Institutions*. New York: MacMillan, 1899.

77. *The Theory of the Leisure Class*. Oxford: Oxford University Press, 2009.

78. Weber, Max. *The Protestant Ethic and the Spirit of Capitalism: The Relationships between Religion and the Economic and Social Life in Modern Culture*. Translated by Talcott Parsons. New York: Charles Scribner's Sons, 1958.

79. Weiner, Annette. *Women of Value, Men of Renown: New Perspectives in Trobriand Exchange*. Austin: University of Texas Press, 1976.

80. Wilkinson, Richard, and Kate Pickett. *The Spirit Level: Why Greater Equality Makes Societies Stronger*. New York: Bloomsbury Press, 2009.

原书作者简介

马塞尔·莫斯生于 1872 年，曾是一位以社会行为研究而闻名的法国社会学家。在获得哲学学位和法律学位后，他开始与他的舅舅、法国社会学之父埃米尔·涂尔干进行合作。其颇具影响力的短篇著作《礼物》首次出版于 1923—1924 年的年刊《社会学年鉴》上，这本期刊由涂尔干于 1898 年创立。

作为一名坚定的社会主义者和政治活动家，莫斯在他撰写和编辑的政治类期刊中分享了他的许多观点，谈到了包括对犹太人的偏见和对政治权力的滥用在内的一系列问题。他于 1950 年在巴黎逝世，享年 77 岁。

本书作者简介

伊丽莎白·惠特克博士在埃默里大学读取了人类学博士学位。她曾在多所美国大学任教，目前是意大利博洛尼亚大学的高级讲师。除了即将出版的一本人类学科普读物之外，她还是《测量母乳：意大利的法西斯主义和产妇医疗化》（安娜堡：密歇根大学出版社，2000 年）一书的作者。

世界名著中的批判性思维

《世界思想宝库钥匙丛书》致力于深入浅出地阐释全世界著名思想家的观点，不论是谁、在何处都能了解到，从而推进批判性思维发展。

《世界思想宝库钥匙丛书》与世界顶尖大学的一流学者合作，为一系列学科中最有影响的著作推出新的分析文本，介绍其观点和影响。在这一不断扩展的系列中，每种选入的著作都代表了历经时间考验的思想典范。通过为这些著作提供必要背景、揭示原作者的学术渊源以及说明这些著作所产生的影响，本系列图书希望让读者以新视角看待这些划时代的经典之作。读者应学会思考、运用并挑战这些著作中的观点，而不是简单接受它们。

ABOUT THE AUTHOR OF THE ORIGINAL WORK

Born in 1872, **Marcel Mauss** was a French sociologist best known for his studies of social behavior. After graduating in philosophy and law, he began working with Émile Durkheim, the 'father of French sociology,' who also happened to be Mauss's uncle. His influential short book *The Gift* was first published in the 1923–24 edition of the annual journal *L'Année Sociologique*, founded by Durkheim in 1898. A committed socialist and political activist, Mauss shared many of his views in writing for—and also editing—political journals. He spoke out on a number of subjects, including prejudice against Jews and the abuse of political power. He died in Paris at the age of 77 in 1950.

ABOUT THE AUTHOR OF THE ANALYSIS

Dr Elizabeth Whitaker holds a PhD in anthropology from Emory University. She has taught at several American universities and is currently a senior lecturer at the Università degli Studi di Bologna, Italy. In addition to a forthcoming book on anthropology for a general audience, she is the author of *Measuring Mamma's Milk: Fascism and the Medicalization of Maternity in Italy* (Ann Arbor: University of Michigan Press, 2000).

ABOUT MACAT
GREAT WORKS FOR CRITICAL THINKING

Macat is focused on making the ideas of the world's great thinkers accessible and comprehensible to everybody, everywhere, in ways that promote the development of enhanced critical thinking skills.

It works with leading academics from the world's top universities to produce new analyses that focus on the ideas and the impact of the most influential works ever written across a wide variety of academic disciplines. Each of the works that sit at the heart of its growing library is an enduring example of great thinking. But by setting them in context — and looking at the influences that shaped their authors, as well as the responses they provoked — Macat encourages readers to look at these classics and game-changers with fresh eyes. Readers learn to think, engage and challenge their ideas, rather than simply accepting them.

批判性思维与《礼物》

首要批判性思维技巧：分析
次要批判性思维技巧：阐释

　　马塞尔·莫斯写于 1925 年的《礼物》是一本有关社会学和人类学的经典著作。他也是现代人类学的奠基人之一。

　　莫斯在《礼物》一书中通过高端分析手法和解释技巧，对多种社会形态下礼物馈赠的形式、意义和结构进行了完美的调查。莫斯和其他许多人都注意到，在多种社会形态中——特别是那些没有货币交换或法制体系的社会——礼物的赠送和接受是根据严格的习俗和不成文的法律进行的。《礼物》一书旨在分析礼物的赠送、接受及回报等一系列活动的方式和时间受哪些因素和结构掌控，并探索其产生的原因。莫斯希望通过他的阐释来探讨礼物交换可能对现代西方文化产生的影响。他的调查表明，在许多文化中，赠送礼物是一种至关重要的结构性力量，它将人们聚集在因礼物交换法则而产生的互惠网络中。简而言之，礼物可以被视为社会的"粘合剂"。

CRITICAL THINKING AND *THE GIFT*

• Primary critical thinking skill: ANALYSIS

• Secondary critical thinking skill: INTERPRETATION

Marcel Mauss's 1925 essay *The Gift* is an enduring classic of sociological and anthropological analysis by a thinker who is one of the founding fathers of modern anthropology.

The Gift exploits Mauss's high-level analytical and interpretative skills to produce a brilliant investigation of the forms, meanings, and structures of gift-giving across a range of societies. Mauss, along with many others, had noted that in a wide range of societies—especially those without monetary exchange or legal structures—gift-giving and receiving was carried out according to strict customs and unwritten laws. What he sought to do in *The Gift* was to analyse the structures that governed how and when gifts were given, received, and reciprocated in order to grasp what implicit and unspoken reasons governed these structures. He also wanted to apply his interpretative skills to asking what such exchanges meant, in order to explore the implications his analysis might have for modern, western cultures. In Mauss's investigations, it became clear that gift-giving is, in many cultures, a crucial structural force, binding people together in a web of reciprocal commitments generated by the laws of gifting. Indeed, he concluded, gifts can be seen as the 'glue' of society.

《世界思想宝库钥匙丛书》简介

《世界思想宝库钥匙丛书》致力于为一系列在各领域产生重大影响的人文社科类经典著作提供独特的学术探讨。每一本读物都不仅仅是原经典著作的内容摘要，而是介绍并深入研究原经典著作的学术渊源、主要观点和历史影响。这一丛书的目的是提供一套学习资料，以促进读者掌握批判性思维，从而更全面、深刻地去理解重要思想。

每一本读物分为 3 个部分：学术渊源、学术思想和学术影响，每个部分下有 4 个小节。这些章节旨在从各个方面研究原经典著作及其反响。

由于独特的体例，每一本读物不但易于阅读，而且另有一项优点：所有读物的编排体例相同，读者在进行某个知识层面的调查或研究时可交叉参阅多本该丛书中的相关读物，从而开启跨领域研究的路径。

为了方便阅读，每本读物最后还列出了术语表和人名表（在书中则以星号 * 标记），此外还有参考文献。

《世界思想宝库钥匙丛书》与剑桥大学合作，理清了批判性思维的要点，即如何通过 6 种技能来进行有效思考。其中 3 种技能让我们能够理解问题，另 3 种技能让我们有能力解决问题。这 6 种技能合称为"批判性思维 PACIER 模式"，它们是：

分析：了解如何建立一个观点；

评估：研究一个观点的优点和缺点；

阐释：对意义所产生的问题加以理解；

创造性思维：提出新的见解，发现新的联系；

解决问题：提出切实有效的解决办法；

理性化思维：创建有说服力的观点。

THE MACAT LIBRARY

The Macat Library is a series of unique academic explorations of seminal works in the humanities and social sciences — books and papers that have had a significant and widely recognised impact on their disciplines. It has been created to serve as much more than just a summary of what lies between the covers of a great book. It illuminates and explores the influences on, ideas of, and impact of that book. Our goal is to offer a learning resource that encourages critical thinking and fosters a better, deeper understanding of important ideas.

Each publication is divided into three Sections: Influences, Ideas, and Impact. Each Section has four Modules. These explore every important facet of the work, and the responses to it.

This Section-Module structure makes a Macat Library book easy to use, but it has another important feature. Because each Macat book is written to the same format, it is possible (and encouraged!) to cross-reference multiple Macat books along the same lines of inquiry or research. This allows the reader to open up interesting interdisciplinary pathways.

To further aid your reading, lists of glossary terms and people mentioned are included at the end of this book (these are indicated by an asterisk [*] throughout) — as well as a list of works cited.

Macat has worked with the University of Cambridge to identify the elements of critical thinking and understand the ways in which six different skills combine to enable effective thinking.

Three allow us to fully understand a problem; three more give us the tools to solve it. Together, these six skills make up the PACIER model of critical thinking. They are:

ANALYSIS — understanding how an argument is built
EVALUATION — exploring the strengths and weaknesses of an argument
INTERPRETATION — understanding issues of meaning
CREATIVE THINKING — coming up with new ideas and fresh connections
PROBLEM-SOLVING — producing strong solutions
REASONING — creating strong arguments

"《世界思想宝库钥匙丛书》提供了独一无二的跨学科学习和研究工具。它介绍那些革新了各自学科研究的经典著作，还邀请全世界一流专家和教育机构进行严谨的分析，为每位读者打开世界顶级教育的大门。"

—— 安德烈亚斯·施莱歇尔，
经济合作与发展组织教育与技能司司长

"《世界思想宝库钥匙丛书》直面大学教育的巨大挑战……他们组建了一支精干而活跃的学者队伍，来推出在研究广度上颇具新意的教学材料。"

—— 布罗尔斯教授、勋爵，剑桥大学前校长

"《世界思想宝库钥匙丛书》的愿景令人赞叹。它通过分析和阐释那些曾深刻影响人类思想以及社会、经济发展的经典文本，提供了新的学习方法。它推动批判性思维，这对于任何社会和经济体来说都是至关重要的。这就是未来的学习方法。"

—— 查尔斯·克拉克阁下，英国前教育大臣

"对于那些影响了各自领域的著作，《世界思想宝库钥匙丛书》能让人们立即了解到围绕那些著作展开的评论性言论，这让该系列图书成为在这些领域从事研究的师生们不可或缺的资源。"

—— 威廉·特朗佐教授，加利福尼亚大学圣地亚哥分校

"Macat offers an amazing first-of-its-kind tool for interdisciplinary learning and research. Its focus on works that transformed their disciplines and its rigorous approach, drawing on the world's leading experts and educational institutions, opens up a world-class education to anyone."

—— Andreas Schleicher, Director for Education and Skills, Organisation for Economic Co-operation and Development

"Macat is taking on some of the major challenges in university education... They have drawn together a strong team of active academics who are producing teaching materials that are novel in the breadth of their approach."

—— Prof Lord Broers, former Vice-Chancellor of the University of Cambridge

"The Macat vision is exceptionally exciting. It focuses upon new modes of learning which analyse and explain seminal texts which have profoundly influenced world thinking and so social and economic development. It promotes the kind of critical thinking which is essential for any society and economy. This is the learning of the future."

—— Rt Hon Charles Clarke, former UK Secretary of State for Education

"The Macat analyses provide immediate access to the critical conversation surrounding the books that have shaped their respective discipline, which will make them an invaluable resource to all of those, students and teachers, working in the field."

—— Prof William Tronzo, University of California at San Diego

The Macat Library
世界思想宝库钥匙丛书

TITLE	中文书名	类别
An Analysis of Arjun Appadurai's *Modernity at Large: Cultural Dimensions of Globalization*	解析阿尔君·阿帕杜莱《消失的现代性：全球化的文化维度》	人类学
An Analysis of Claude Lévi-Strauss's *Structural Anthropology*	解析克劳德·列维-斯特劳斯《结构人类学》	人类学
An Analysis of Marcel Mauss's *The Gift*	解析马塞尔·莫斯《礼物》	人类学
An Analysis of Jared M. Diamond's *Guns, Germs, and Steel: The Fate of Human Societies*	解析贾雷德·M.戴蒙德《枪炮、病菌与钢铁：人类社会的命运》	人类学
An Analysis of Clifford Geertz's *The Interpretation of Cultures*	解析克利福德·格尔茨《文化的解释》	人类学
An Analysis of Philippe Ariès's *Centuries of Childhood: A Social History of Family Life*	解析菲力浦·阿利埃斯《儿童的世纪：旧制度下的儿童和家庭生活》	人类学
An Analysis of W. Chan Kim & Renée Mauborgne's *Blue Ocean Strategy*	解析金伟灿/勒妮·莫博涅《蓝海战略》	商业
An Analysis of John P. Kotter's *Leading Change*	解析约翰·P.科特《领导变革》	商业
An Analysis of Michael E. Porter's *Competitive Strategy: Techniques for Analyzing Industries and Competitors*	解析迈克尔·E.波特《竞争战略：分析产业和竞争对手的技术》	商业
An Analysis of Jean Lave & Etienne Wenger's *Situated Learning: Legitimate Peripheral Participation*	解析琼·莱夫/艾蒂纳·温格《情境学习：合法的边缘性参与》	商业
An Analysis of Douglas McGregor's *The Human Side of Enterprise*	解析道格拉斯·麦格雷戈《企业的人性面》	商业
An Analysis of Milton Friedman's *Capitalism and Freedom*	解析米尔顿·弗里德曼《资本主义与自由》	商业
An Analysis of Ludwig von Mises's *The Theory of Money and Credit*	解析路德维希·冯·米塞斯《货币和信用理论》	经济学
An Analysis of Adam Smith's *The Wealth of Nations*	解析亚当·斯密《国富论》	经济学
An Analysis of Thomas Piketty's *Capital in the Twenty-First Century*	解析托马斯·皮凯蒂《21世纪资本论》	经济学
An Analysis of Nassim Nicholas Taleb's *The Black Swan: The Impact of the Highly Improbable*	解析纳西姆·尼古拉斯·塔勒布《黑天鹅：如何应对不可预知的未来》	经济学
An Analysis of Ha-Joon Chang's *Kicking Away the Ladder*	解析张夏准《富国陷阱：发达国家为何踢开梯子》	经济学
An Analysis of Thomas Robert Malthus's *An Essay on the Principle of Population*	解析托马斯·罗伯特·马尔萨斯《人口论》	经济学

An Analysis of John Maynard Keynes's *The General Theory of Employment, Interest and Money*	解析约翰·梅纳德·凯恩斯《就业、利息和货币通论》	经济学
An Analysis of Milton Friedman's *The Role of Monetary Policy*	解析米尔顿·弗里德曼《货币政策的作用》	经济学
An Analysis of Burton G. Malkiel's *A Random Walk Down Wall Street*	解析伯顿·G.马尔基尔《漫步华尔街》	经济学
An Analysis of Friedrich A. Hayek's *The Road to Serfdom*	解析弗里德里希·A.哈耶克《通往奴役之路》	经济学
An Analysis of Charles P. Kindleberger's *Manias, Panics, and Crashes: A History of Financial Crises*	解析查尔斯·P.金德尔伯格《疯狂、惊恐和崩溃：金融危机史》	经济学
An Analysis of Amartya Sen's *Development as Freedom*	解析阿马蒂亚·森《以自由看待发展》	经济学
An Analysis of Rachel Carson's *Silent Spring*	解析蕾切尔·卡森《寂静的春天》	地理学
An Analysis of Charles Darwin's *On the Origin of Species: by Means of Natural Selection, or The Preservation of Favoured Races in the Struggle for Life*	解析查尔斯·达尔文《物种起源》	地理学
An Analysis of World Commission on Environment and Development's *The Brundtland Report: Our Common Future*	解析世界环境与发展委员会《布伦特兰报告：我们共同的未来》	地理学
An Analysis of James E. Lovelock's *Gaia: A New Look at Life on Earth*	解析詹姆斯·E.拉伍洛克《盖娅：地球生命的新视野》	地理学
An Analysis of Paul Kennedy's *The Rise and Fall of the Great Powers: Economic Change and Military Conflict from 1500–2000*	解析保罗·肯尼迪《大国的兴衰：1500—2000年的经济变革与军事冲突》	历史
An Analysis of Janet L. Abu-Lughod's *Before European Hegemony: The World System A. D. 1250–1350*	解析珍妮特·L.阿布-卢格霍德《欧洲霸权之前：1250—1350年的世界体系》	历史
An Analysis of Alfred W. Crosby's *The Columbian Exchange: Biological and Cultural Consequences of 1492*	解析艾尔弗雷德·W.克罗斯比《哥伦布大交换：1492年以后的生物影响和文化冲击》	历史
An Analysis of Tony Judt's *Postwar: A History of Europe since 1945*	解析托尼·朱特《战后欧洲史》	历史
An Analysis of Richard J. Evans's *In Defence of History*	解析理查德·J.艾文斯《捍卫历史》	历史
An Analysis of Eric Hobsbawm's *The Age of Revolution: Europe 1789–1848*	解析艾瑞克·霍布斯鲍姆《革命的年代：欧洲1789—1848年》	历史

An Analysis of Roland Barthes's *Mythologies*	解析罗兰·巴特《神话学》	文学与批判理论
An Analysis of Simone de Beauvoir's *The Second Sex*	解析西蒙娜·德·波伏娃《第二性》	文学与批判理论
An Analysis of Edward W. Said's *Orientalism*	解析爱德华·W.萨义德《东方主义》	文学与批判理论
An Analysis of Virginia Woolf's *A Room of One's Own*	解析弗吉尼亚·伍尔芙《一间自己的房间》	文学与批判理论
An Analysis of Judith Butler's *Gender Trouble*	解析朱迪斯·巴特勒《性别麻烦》	文学与批判理论
An Analysis of Ferdinand de Saussure's *Course in General Linguistics*	解析费尔迪南·德·索绪尔《普通语言学教程》	文学与批判理论
An Analysis of Susan Sontag's *On Photography*	解析苏珊·桑塔格《论摄影》	文学与批判理论
An Analysis of Walter Benjamin's *The Work of Art in the Age of Mechanical Reproduction*	解析瓦尔特·本雅明《机械复制时代的艺术作品》	文学与批判理论
An Analysis of W. E. B. Du Bois's *The Souls of Black Folk*	解析W.E.B.杜波依斯《黑人的灵魂》	文学与批判理论
An Analysis of Plato's *The Republic*	解析柏拉图《理想国》	哲学
An Analysis of Plato's *Symposium*	解析柏拉图《会饮篇》	哲学
An Analysis of Aristotle's *Metaphysics*	解析亚里士多德《形而上学》	哲学
An Analysis of Aristotle's *Nicomachean Ethics*	解析亚里士多德《尼各马可伦理学》	哲学
An Analysis of Immanuel Kant's *Critique of Pure Reason*	解析伊曼努尔·康德《纯粹理性批判》	哲学
An Analysis of Ludwig Wittgenstein's *Philosophical Investigations*	解析路德维希·维特根斯坦《哲学研究》	哲学
An Analysis of G. W. F. Hegel's *Phenomenology of Spirit*	解析G.W.F.黑格尔《精神现象学》	哲学
An Analysis of Baruch Spinoza's *Ethics*	解析巴鲁赫·斯宾诺莎《伦理学》	哲学
An Analysis of Hannah Arendt's *The Human Condition*	解析汉娜·阿伦特《人的境况》	哲学
An Analysis of G. E. M. Anscombe's *Modern Moral Philosophy*	解析G.E.M.安斯康姆《现代道德哲学》	哲学
An Analysis of David Hume's *An Enquiry Concerning Human Understanding*	解析大卫·休谟《人类理解研究》	哲学

An Analysis of Søren Kierkegaard's *Fear and Trembling*	解析索伦·克尔凯郭尔《恐惧与战栗》	哲学
An Analysis of René Descartes's *Meditations on First Philosophy*	解析勒内·笛卡尔《第一哲学沉思录》	哲学
An Analysis of Friedrich Nietzsche's *On the Genealogy of Morality*	解析弗里德里希·尼采《论道德的谱系》	哲学
An Analysis of Gilbert Ryle's *The Concept of Mind*	解析吉尔伯特·赖尔《心的概念》	哲学
An Analysis of Thomas Kuhn's *The Structure of Scientific Revolutions*	解析托马斯·库恩《科学革命的结构》	哲学
An Analysis of John Stuart Mill's *Utilitarianism*	解析约翰·斯图亚特·穆勒《功利主义》	哲学
An Analysis of Aristotle's *Politics*	解析亚里士多德《政治学》	政治学
An Analysis of Niccolò Machiavelli's *The Prince*	解析尼科洛·马基雅维利《君主论》	政治学
An Analysis of Karl Marx's *Capital*	解析卡尔·马克思《资本论》	政治学
An Analysis of Benedict Anderson's *Imagined Communities*	解析本尼迪克特·安德森《想象的共同体》	政治学
An Analysis of Samuel P. Huntington's *The Clash of Civilizations and the Remaking of World Order*	解析塞缪尔·P.亨廷顿《文明的冲突与世界秩序的重建》	政治学
An Analysis of Alexis de Tocqueville's *Democracy in America*	解析阿列克西·德·托克维尔《论美国的民主》	政治学
An Analysis of John A. Hobson's *Imperialism: A Study*	解析约翰·A.霍布森《帝国主义》	政治学
An Analysis of Thomas Paine's *Common Sense*	解析托马斯·潘恩《常识》	政治学
An Analysis of John Rawls's *A Theory of Justice*	解析约翰·罗尔斯《正义论》	政治学
An Analysis of Francis Fukuyama's *The End of History and the Last Man*	解析弗朗西斯·福山《历史的终结与最后的人》	政治学
An Analysis of John Locke's *Two Treatises of Government*	解析约翰·洛克《政府论》	政治学
An Analysis of Sun Tzu's *The Art of War*	解析孙武《孙子兵法》	政治学
An Analysis of Henry Kissinger's *World Order: Reflections on the Character of Nations and the Course of History*	解析亨利·基辛格《世界秩序》	政治学
An Analysis of Jean-Jacques Rousseau's *The Social Contract*	解析让-雅克·卢梭《社会契约论》	政治学

An Analysis of Odd Arne Westad's *The Global Cold War: Third World Interventions and the Making of Our Times*	解析文安立《全球冷战：美苏对第三世界的干涉与当代世界的形成》	政治学
An Analysis of Sigmund Freud's *The Interpretation of Dreams*	解析西格蒙德·弗洛伊德《梦的解析》	心理学
An Analysis of William James' *The Principles of Psychology*	解析威廉·詹姆斯《心理学原理》	心理学
An Analysis of Philip Zimbardo's *The Lucifer Effect*	解析菲利普·津巴多《路西法效应》	心理学
An Analysis of Leon Festinger's *A Theory of Cognitive Dissonance*	解析利昂·费斯汀格《认知失调论》	心理学
An Analysis of Richard H. Thaler & Cass R. Sunstein's *Nudge: Improving Decisions about Health, Wealth, and Happiness*	解析理查德·H.泰勒/卡斯·R.桑斯坦《助推：如何做出有关健康、财富和幸福的更优决策》	心理学
An Analysis of Gordon Allport's *The Nature of Prejudice*	解析高尔登·奥尔波特《偏见的本质》	心理学
An Analysis of Steven Pinker's *The Better Angels of Our Nature: Why Violence Has Declined*	解析斯蒂芬·平克《人性中的善良天使：暴力为什么会减少》	心理学
An Analysis of Stanley Milgram's *Obedience to Authority*	解析斯坦利·米尔格拉姆《对权威的服从》	心理学
An Analysis of Betty Friedan's *The Feminine Mystique*	解析贝蒂·弗里丹《女性的奥秘》	心理学
An Analysis of David Riesman's *The Lonely Crowd: A Study of the Changing American Character*	解析大卫·理斯曼《孤独的人群：美国人社会性格演变之研究》	社会学
An Analysis of Franz Boas's *Race, Language and Culture*	解析弗朗兹·博厄斯《种族、语言与文化》	社会学
An Analysis of Pierre Bourdieu's *Outline of a Theory of Practice*	解析皮埃尔·布尔迪厄《实践理论大纲》	社会学
An Analysis of Max Weber's *The Protestant Ethic and the Spirit of Capitalism*	解析马克斯·韦伯《新教伦理与资本主义精神》	社会学
An Analysis of Jane Jacobs's *The Death and Life of Great American Cities*	解析简·雅各布斯《美国大城市的死与生》	社会学
An Analysis of C. Wright Mills's *The Sociological Imagination*	解析C.赖特·米尔斯《社会学的想象力》	社会学
An Analysis of Robert E. Lucas Jr.'s *Why Doesn't Capital Flow from Rich to Poor Countries?*	解析小罗伯特·E.卢卡斯《为何资本不从富国流向穷国？》	社会学

An Analysis of Émile Durkheim's *On Suicide*	解析埃米尔·迪尔凯姆《自杀论》	社会学
An Analysis of Eric Hoffer's *The True Believer: Thoughts on the Nature of Mass Movements*	解析埃里克·霍弗《狂热分子：群众运动圣经》	社会学
An Analysis of Jared M. Diamond's *Collapse: How Societies Choose to Fail or Survive*	解析贾雷德·M.戴蒙德《大崩溃：社会如何选择兴亡》	社会学
An Analysis of Michel Foucault's *The History of Sexuality Vol. 1: The Will to Knowledge*	解析米歇尔·福柯《性史（第一卷）：求知意志》	社会学
An Analysis of Michel Foucault's *Discipline and Punish*	解析米歇尔·福柯《规训与惩罚》	社会学
An Analysis of Richard Dawkins's *The Selfish Gene*	解析理查德·道金斯《自私的基因》	社会学
An Analysis of Antonio Gramsci's *Prison Notebooks*	解析安东尼奥·葛兰西《狱中札记》	社会学
An Analysis of Augustine's *Confessions*	解析奥古斯丁《忏悔录》	神学
An Analysis of C. S. Lewis's *The Abolition of Man*	解析 C. S. 路易斯《人之废》	神学

图书在版编目（CIP）数据

解析马塞尔·莫斯《礼物》: 汉、英 / 伊丽莎白·惠特克（Elizabeth Whitaker）著
韩蒙译. —上海: 上海外语教育出版社, 2020
（世界思想宝库钥匙丛书）
ISBN 978-7-5446-6448-6

Ⅰ.①解… Ⅱ.①伊… ②韩… Ⅲ.①社会人类学—研究—汉、英 Ⅳ.①C912.4

中国版本图书馆CIP数据核字（2020）第079929号

This Chinese-English bilingual edition of *An Analysis of Marcel Mauss's* The Gift is published by
arrangement with Macat International Limited.
Licensed for sale throughout the world.

本书汉英双语版由Macat国际有限公司授权上海外语教育出版社有限公司出版。
供在全世界范围内发行、销售。

图字：09 – 2018 – 549

出版发行：上海外语教育出版社
　　　　　（上海外国语大学内）　邮编：200083
电　　话：021-65425300（总机）
电子邮箱：bookinfo@sflep.com.cn
网　　址：http://www.sflep.com
责任编辑：王叶涵

印　　刷：上海叶大印务发展有限公司
开　　本：890×1240　1/32　印张 6.875　字数 142千字
版　　次：2020 年 8月第 1版　　2020 年 8月第 1次印刷
印　　数：2 100 册

书　　号：ISBN 978-7-5446-6448-6
定　　价：30.00 元
　　　　本版图书如有印装质量问题, 可向本社调换
　　　　质量服务热线：4008-213-263　电子邮箱：editorial@sflep.com